BY JAY LEACH

How Should We Then Live?
Behold the Man
The Blood Runs Through It
Drawn Away
Give Me Jesus
A Light unto My Path
Grace that Saves
The Narrow Way
Radical Restoration in the Church
Manifestation of the true Children of God
According to Pattern
Battle Cry
Is There Not A Cause?
We Would See Jesus
According to Pattern 2nd Edition
The Apostolic Rising

THE
APOSTOLIC
RISING

THE RESTORATION OF THE
APOSTOLIC MINISTRIES
(Functions)

JAY LEACH

Order this book online at www.trafford.com
or email orders@trafford.com

Most Trafford titles are also available at major online book retailers.

Print information available on the last page.

ISBN: 978-1-6987-0577-4 (sc)
ISBN: 978-1-6987-0576-7 (e)

Scripture taken from The Holy Bible, King James Version. Public Domain

The New King James version of the Bible (copyright 1982 by
Thomas Nelson Inc), unless otherwise noted.

The Answer, the New Century version (copyright 2003 by Thomas Nelson Inc.)

Zondervan NIV Study Bible (copyright 2002 by the Zondervan Corp.)

The Spirit-filled Life Bible (copyright 2003 by Thomas Nelson Inc.)

Trafford rev. 02/05/2021

 www.trafford.com
North America & international
toll-free: 844-688-6899 (USA & Canada)
fax: 812 355 4082

*"But we all with unveiled face, beholding as in a mirror
the glory of the Lord,
are being transformed into the same image
from glory to glory,
just as by the Spirit of the Lord."*

1 Corinthians 3:18)

*That I will pour out of My Spirit
on all flesh;
Your sons and your daughters
shall prophesy.
Your young men shall see visions,
Your old men shall dream dreams.
And on My menservants and on
My maidservants
I will pour out My Spirit in those
days;
and they shall prophesy.
I will show wonders in heaven
above
and signs in the earth beneath;
blood and fire and vapor of smoke.
The sun shall be turned into
darkness,
And the moon into blood,
Before the coming of the great and
awesome day of the LORD.
And it shall come to pass
That whoever calls on the name of
The LORD
Shall be saved.*

Acts 2:17-21

CONTENTS

SECTION IV
APOSTOLIC TIMES

INTRODUCTION

The Blood of Jesus formed a very deep demarcation line amongst humanity from the very beginning. So, Satan is able to cause much division and distortion in the Christian Community and society as well, concerning this subject? People are confused and full of fear because they lack "the knowledge of the truth!" The unsaved are blind to the truth of the rejection of the blood of Jesus. Since the beginning of man's "sin" in the Garden of Eden, *two religions* have run parallel to each other and they show up very identifiably in the sacrifices of Cain and Abel (see Genesis 4). Onward throughout the Scripture we see Satan's footprints as he spreads a [bloodless institutional religion] in contrast to [Christ's blood in Christianity]. However, the spiritual significance of the sacrifice goes back to God shedding the blood of two animals [probably lambs] to cover Adam and Eve's [sinful] nakedness. I am sure that Adam passed this lesson on to both of his sons [Cain being the oldest]. However, semblance of their interpretation and actions reverberate throughout the Christian community today: Abel's blood sacrifice is characterized by what God requires; and Cain's bloodless sacrifice is characterized by what humanity is willing to offer God. In order to get a clearer understanding of the situation wherein true believers are faced with the enemy and locked in death-defying spiritual warfare involving "the lie" as opposed to "true truth." As long as Satan can persuade believers **to drift from the standards of God's Word,** [mainly through societal influence and conformity to the world] then he is winning *the spiritual* *battle* within them and quenching the power and operations of the Holy Spirit in their lives. Once weakened, Satan tempts your old sinful nature to look to **self** for power and fulfillment and become *independent in these Last Days*. When Satan is allowed to be successful at this, it weakens our access to the only *source* of deliverance from the law and our old sinful nature – *the blood of Jesus*. The Scripture indicates that "to know the true truth" we must go back to the beginning found only in the Holy Bible. In Romans 5, the Apostle Paul takes us back to the beginning of human history [emphasis added throughout]:

> *"Therefore, just as "through one man, sin entered the world and death through sin, and thus death spread to all men, because all sinned. But the free gift [righteousness] is not like the offense. For if by the one man's offense many died, much more the grace of God and the gift by the grace of the one Man, Jesus Christ, abounded to many"* (Romans 5:12, 15).

Therefore, just as through Adam sin entered the world, along with death and judgment, both of which are now universal experiences (see Genesis 2:17; 3:19). In the phrase "all have sinned," Paul does not mean "sin at some time in life," thus referring to individual sins. He is referring to the one sin of Adam that brought death upon us all. The result is spiritual and physical death for everyone. After sinning Adam and Eve hid themselves from God, by trying to cover themselves [sin and guilt] with fig leaves. God through His great love for them killed two animals [shedding innocent blood] and took their skins to make tunics to cover Adam and Eve's nakedness. From Adam we all inherited his sin nature. Paul continues,

> *"For if by the one man's offense death reigned through the one, much more those who receive abundance of grace and of the gift of righteousness will reign in life through the One, Jesus Christ"* (v. 17).

The *second* Adam, Jesus Christ, was the perfect sinless, **[blood]** sacrifice to take away sin and bring resurrection and eternal life to those who believe in Him, the true [Truth and Life]. Jesus wants us to partner with Him to restore that which was lost. This book may not be for you. In the past, it was not for me either. It is my prayer in writing it; that it will communicate well enough what I want to say about the desperate need for *physical* and *spiritual reform* in our local churches. Reform means change! We are the only army that allow our soldiers to engage the enemy in a spiritual warfare (generation after generation) without General level leadership in this case, [Apostolic ministry].

Apostles were *sent* to establish the Kingdom <u>in the hearts of people and to establish churches throughout the world.</u> They were given the power of the Holy Spirit to help them fulfill their mission. If the commission is apostolic, that means only *sent ones* can fulfill it. Every believer must have this apostolic dimension to be a part of fulfilling the Great Commission. Listen, this **does not make** everyone an apostle – but everyone can *be apostolic*. Therefore, the local church needs to be an apostolic church – if it is to fulfill its mission. The vast majority of churches agree that they are "called out," but so few accept to be "sent out" as well! You will see the importance and understand *why the Church has struggled* in its attempt to fulfill the Great Commission. The purpose in writing this book is to bring understanding to the whole Body of Christ – what it means "to be sent." That way, each of us may then go forth and fulfill what God has called, anointed, and equipped us to do.

To be apostolic revolves around the concept of being sent by Christ through the power of the Holy Spirit. I repeat, only Spirit-filled sent ones can fulfill the Great Commission. Only Spirit-filled sent ones will be *able to overcome the impossible odds* that stand in the way of being able to say, "Mission accomplished." The church cannot succeed without *strongly operating* in this apostolic dimension.

Apostolic Ministry (see Ephesians 4:11,13) is essential in the local churches of each generation for proper alignment with the will of God toward accomplishing Christ's *assigned* Kingdom missions (see Matthew 28:19-20). Included would be a review ministries and procedures for making necessary changes to ensure that local churches remain relevant to the *spiritual* and *physical* needs of the people; and be alive and alert to hear what the Spirit is saying to the churches today. Sadly, many local churches will continue using forms, methods, irrelevant programs, and ministries based on the church founders' traditions passed down a number of generations earlier. Often the strongman in these areas are spirits of religion and tradition among the leadership. It grieves my heart to be so critical of the church that nurtured me as a youngster and imparted the faith to me, that in spite of my failures, and shortcomings through the years continues to confirm my purpose and calling.

I grew up in the home of a bivocational pastor, my father, whose father and grandfather were preachers reaching back to the "invisible church" of the (slaves) and later the early African American Institutional Baptist Church tradition. Pastoral ministry and Bible teaching have been the life of my wife and I for the past 38 years since retiring from the U.S. Army. However, we found it increasingly difficult to feel at home in the institutional traditional church. Today it lacks spiritual purpose and missional life – operating mainly through a strict church tradition and narrow theology, which is backed-up by an institutional resistance to change.

I am talking about a church culture that has largely forsaken God's New Covenant and Christ's mission through His body, the church to fulfill His kingdom mandates.[1] The church has depreciated over the past two thousand years, due to humanity's substitution of their own standards for biblical standards. Their desired standards would make the church a sort of country club where religious people hang out with others who think, dress, behave, vote, participate in the same secret lodges, fraternal organizations, and *believe* like them in [institutional religion]. Having left that part of the church some years ago, this book will further separate us from many people in the institutional church who will never understand what or who led us to do what we do. Yet, I often converse with people like me in the church, who in their own church experiences want to write a story different from the one they are now a part of. My work carries me into various congregations, and meetings with various denominational church leaders every year. I pastor and teach weekly classes at the Bread of Life Bible Institute and Church. I also participate in various seminars, workshops, and consult with leaders across denominational lines.

In every endeavor, we run into an increasing number of people who are expressing foundational doubts about the spiritual life of their local church. I spoke with a young pastor some weeks ago, who told me he is sick and tired of being sick and tired! He exclaimed, "Why am I still doing this?" He is just getting started – I am sure that some of us are asking that same question after many years of investment.

Today, the Church is facing the greatest challenge that it has ever known. There is an alarming increase in sin and lawlessness of every

---

[1]   Matthew 22:37-40; 28:19-20

kind. There is an amazing increase of satanic counterfeit Christians, gospels, spiritual gifts and signs all over the world. This is happening at a time when much of the leadership in the churches in America are hiding the *key to knowledge* of the Holy Spirit, and His gifts, and ministries by willful omission, through false forms, traditions, and skeptical and untrue expositions. Thus, leaving many Christians with no defense against Satan's end-time onslaught of demonic deceptions and other spiritual attacks. Additionally, parts of the church are unwilling to encourage the operation of the Holy Spirit's empowering gifts for fear of creating disorder and their own loss of prestige and power.

Spiritual gifts are God's acts in the world, and whenever the manifestations of God's power and purpose through the manifestation of spiritual gifts *were lacking,* there was enormous backsliding and apostasy. We are now experiencing this widespread in local churches today.

Hopefully, this book will help you, and give you hope. This book is not for you if you are content with traditional and institutional religion. Yet, if you are convinced that God wants you in present truth and that He is not through with you, then you should read it.

This book is divided into four sections:

Section I: The results of Adam's sin [alienation]
Section II: Obedience is better than sacrifice [obedience]
Section III: The Apostolic Rising [service]
Section IV: Apostolic Times [faith]

Satan's time is short

The Body of Christ needs a fresh awakening of present truth. We need it because our generation is living in a time of powerful demonic seduction and deception. Jesus warned that such days would come "days in which Satan would attempt to deceive even the very elect of God." Today we are seeing Jesus' words come to pass, as humanity faces an overwhelming flood of deceptions and temptations, the magnitude *unknown* to any past generation.

It appears that the devil has gained control of much of the media today as satellites beam pornography into homes all over the world. Sadly, much of the technology meant to improve our lives has been hijacked and used as open floodgates for evil, and society has been seduced with a ferocity never seen before. The atmosphere is saturated with every form of media to feed lusts, encourage promiscuity and destroy every fiber of morality. In the process the devil is breaking up biblical marriage and the family.

The counterpunch

Tragically, many Christians are being swept up into a demonic web of sensuality. Believers who have played around with secret sins are now finding themselves in a drastic battle for their *souls*. Our prayer lines and deliverance ministries receive numerous calls and requests for help from distraught *believers* who describe being in sinful bondages. They speak of *life-controlling habits* in their own lives and their loved ones: habits such as drugs, alcohol, lust, pornography, adultery, fornication, homosexuality, anger, bitterness, lottery, and stealing. No matter what their struggle is they all have this in common: They are bound, lured into slavery by a besetting sin. They have cried prayed diligently sought pastoral counseling and others, yet nothing seems to set them free. They end up falling back into their sin, and heavy burden of guilt. Paul described this *bondage of the flesh* in Romans 7. He or she is unable to move into the *spiritual freedom* of Romans 8:1, where power over the dominion of sin is revealed. The Word of God promises hope, and empowerment to win over temptations and lusts if you, the believer:

- Fear God
- Hate your sin and repent
- Grieve over bondage of habitual lust
- Cry out to the Lord for mercy and deliverance from Satan's snare
- Feel helpless over your lack of power

I must submit to God my helplessness toward extracting the sin in my own natural power. All indwelling sin can be stripped of its dominion over you through the indwelling Holy Spirit. Likewise, if your church practices institutional religion, which denies the power, perhaps you are in the wrong church. The apostolic ministries of Ephesians 4:11] given to the Church by Christ Himself, the Head of the Church – to be functioning – for how long?

"till we all come to the unity of the faith and of the knowledge of the Son of God, to a perfect man, to the measure of the stature of the fullness of Christ."

As we have opportunity, we must stop discussing whether or not the ministries of the apostle, prophet, and teacher are to exist in the body of Christ today and turn our attention to the crucial need for their *functioning* alongside the evangelist, and pastor. It is time to stop trying to justify a past non-biblical position and grasp an understanding of the apostolic and begin to vigorously contend for "present truth." They are true biblical expressions of the apostolic functions that Christ is restoring to the churches for the Last Days. Hear what the Spirit is saying to the churches! Everyone who believes and receives Jesus as their personal Savior *receives* the Holy Spirit (Romans 5:5). This is the major difference between Christianity and other beliefs and religions.

Though there is much self or Satan-based abuse of these biblical titles, it is past time for the apostolic Spiritual leadership of the local Christian Communities to expose the counterfeits, and non-spiritual hierarchies in the churches by reinstituting the true blood-washed, Spirit-filled, Bible-believing and relevant [Ephesians 4:11] ministries immediately!

"God is raising up a new breed of believers [a new wineskin] – who will prophesy, pray, preach, teach, bind and loose."

Jay R. Leach

These believers *know that* no weapon formed against us shall prosper. *When* the enemy comes in like a flood, the *Spirit of the Lord will* raise up a standard against him (Isaiah 59:19). Even though Church history has been established and is available in print – so is the history of the Apostolic Church and the apostles, prophets, evangelists, pastors, and teachers in the New Testament, who are to function until He returns. God is raising up [*today*] a new apostolic generation [new wineskin] who will preach "Christ" out of *a personal encounter and revelation of who He really is.* When these anointed vessels enter cities, towns and churches, the saints will become convinced that these apostolic ministers are more *concerned about their maturity in Christ—than they are about receiving an honorarium and moving on.* The Holy Spirit will anoint their declarations and *restore awe and love for the Son of God as they minister.* I hope to show you in this book how that gloriously takes place. It has been said, "Because a thing has been practiced for 2000 years does not mean it is right – likewise because a thing has not been practiced for 2000 years does not mean it is wrong!" Amen?

Jay R. Leach
Fayetteville, NC

SECTION I

THE RESULTS OF ADAM'S SIN

(ALIENATION)

CHAPTER ONE

FROM THE BEGINNING
[A L E I N A T I O N]

And the Lord God commanded the man saying, "Of every tree of the garden you may freely eat; but of the tree of the knowledge of good and evil you shall not eat, for in the day that you eat of it you shall surely die" (Genesis 2:16, 17).

Much debate has been leveled by various groups concerning the first eleven chapters of the Bible. One says, do not take the chapters literally, another claims they are derived from Greek mythology, etc. However, we do take them literally. If Satan could get rid of these eleven chapters, the rest of the Bible would not make sense.

Another myth denying these chapters involves the theory of evolution which caused much contention in the 1800's that says: man evolved [a good man] from some oozy bog out of a pagan past; and ever since that emergence, the human race has continually improved itself and thus gave rise to the "bloodless sacrifice" of *institutional religion* which is consuming much of the American church today. We will address this topic further in later chapters.

The true story

The true story of human origin is found in Genesis 1:26, *Then God said, "Let us make man in Our image, according to Our likeness; let them have dominion over the fish of the sea, and over the birds of the air, and over the cattle, over all the earth, and over every creeping thing that creeps on the earth."*

The Bible begins, *"In the beginning God created the heaven and the earth."* Creation marks the absolute beginning of the temporal and material world. On the sixth day of creation in contrast to animals in verses 20 and 24 where God said, *"Let the waters bring forth and let the earth bring forth,"* He now says, ***"Let us make man in Our image, according to Our likeness."*** Notice all others reproduce after "their kind," but man is the only one made in the image of God and reproduces in that image; and though marred by sin, the image is still there (see Genesis 3:5).

In creation God placed a great chasm between man and beast, for only man has the capacity for:

- Personal relationship with his or her Creator
- Eternal life
- Fellowship
- Moral discernment
- Self-consciousness
- Speech
- Worship

God created man innocent, but not righteous; therefore, he had a choice of obedience as seen in (Genesis 2:16-17).

> *"And the Lord God commanded the man saying, "Of every tree of the Garden you may freely eat; but of the tree of the knowledge of good and evil, you shall not eat, for in the day that you eat of it you shall surely die."*

The fall of man

Adam and Eve chose, but it was the wrong choice. As a result of their choice man has suffered from the **"fall."**

- Human nature is evil.

- The nations are raging.
- The world is in a mess.
- Society is deteriorating.
- Cultures are mingled.
- Religion has become simply what man is willing to offer God.

In many quarters of our society, the church is considered non-essential having been uprooted by science and reason as we have seen during the COVID-19 epidemic and the recent coup attempt. The Scripture says, God is not mocked, whatsoever, a man sows that shall he also reap" (Galatians 6:7).

We find the reason for this condition [Satan and sin] and the solution to it [Jesus Christ and salvation] in Genesis 3:15! Lurking in the Garden was Satan, the father of lies. Where did he come from? He was created one of God's highest angels named Lucifer which means "morning star" or *"light bearer."* He led an angelic rebellion. He was the original sinner. Isaiah recorded Satan's fall (Isaiah 14:12). For Satan said in his heart:

- I will ascend into heaven.
- I will exalt my throne above the stars of God.
- I will sit also upon the mount of the congregation.
- I will ascend above the heights of the clouds.
- I will be like the Highest.

In Genesis 3:1-4, we read, *Now the serpent was more subtle than any beast of the field which the Lord God had made. And he said unto the woman, Yea, hath God said, <u>Ye shall not eat of every tree in the garden?</u> And the woman said unto the serpent, we may eat of the fruit of the trees of the garden: But of the fruit of the tree, which is in the midst of the garden, God hath said, <u>Ye shall not eat of it, **neither shall ye touch it, lest ye die**</u>. And the serpent said unto the woman, <u>Ye shall not surely die.</u>"* [KJV] She took away the word *"freely"* and changed **thou shalt surely die** from the truth of God's Word and she added to His Word: **shall not touch it lest we die.** Emphasis added.

Sin entered

The serpent was a creature made by God but used of Satan (see John 8:44; 1 John 3:8; Revelation 12:9; 20:2). Eve proved to be under the influence of Satan. We can learn much from Eve's encounter with the serpent in that Satan uses the same tricks today in our local churches. Notice how Satan deceitfully got Eve to add and subtract from what God had commanded. His specialty is to get people to change truth into lies. The result is doubt. Doubt negates faith. Notice his approach, "Has God said?"

Adam and Eve were disobedient; and afterward, sewed fig leaves together to cover their nakedness and they shamefully hid from God. Their next downward step was to begin to doubt God's sincerity. Once doubt sets in then doubt of truth comes. Adam forgot that he owed his existence to God, the Creator and Sustainer of all things. This made Adam and Eve totally dependent creatures. He nor she is self-existent and thus humanity could not then nor today be independent. It is in God that "we live and move and have our being" (see Acts 17:23-31).

Humans are moral beings

God created man with a free-will. Freewill makes human beings moral and therefore *responsible*. Just as God created the angelic hosts as beings with free will, having the power of choice, so God created man with the power of choice. Man is not a robot, nor is he a machine or will-less. God desired that man would respond to Him willingly and freely. That necessitated man to have a free will to choose. He loved so much that He wrapped Himself in a human body, came and died on the cross – for us. We sinned in a human body so, He sacrificed Himself in a human body and rose from the dead – so that we could live. What love!

God placed within human beings a conscience which gives them a moral sense, distinguishing right from wrong in relation to a known law. Conscience is fallible, for since man's *fall*, knowledge has been perverted through sin, it does not form a perfect basis for judgment. The *only* true standard for conscience is the truth of God's Word [the Bible] *as revealed* by the Holy Spirit. However, only those who have been born again, from above have this access to the Spirit. The Spirit brings the conscience in line with the infallible Word of God (see Romans 9:1).

God is love and love must have an object which can reciprocate that love (see I John 4:16-19). God's answer was the creation of man. Man is a being with a will and intelligence; capable of *choosing to love*. Human beings were created by love, for love, and to reciprocate love. Without such love the human heart remains empty and cold.

Therefore, on the Cain side of the "blood line" came "rationalization."[2] One such conclusion is that in the fall, man became deprived except for his mind or intellect. And therefore, the intellect enables man to discern right and wrong through the five senses. However, with Creation put on the back burner today we have moved from the modern world to the postmodern world and from a Christian era to a post-Christian era. The COVID-19 epidemic has made that obvious in the government's moving of the church to non-essential status in this crisis. The Bible and truth have also been routed as postmodernism thrives on chaos as we are witnessing across this country. It strives for a world in which everything is *relative,* where there is no *truth* and perception alone is *reality.* Since God's eternal truth has no place in postmodernism – supposedly, science, psychology, philosophy and rationalization are the determinants.

Born in academia, postmodernism has taken control of all levels of the educational systems, government, the home and marriage and the family. It is apparent that this whole debacle is a strategy of Satan, the prince of this world, working through atheism and secular humanism to dismantle Christianity and I believe to destroy this nation and the rest of the West.

A few years ago, the mayor of Houston Texas directed the pastors of some of their leading churches to submit a copy of their sermon manuscript to insure nothing in it referred to homosexuality – well that did not wash because pastors from all over America went into a frenzy some boarding airplanes immediately bound for Houston. The mayor backed down. For the next couple of years our "religious freedom" seemed to be eking-away as Christians in businesses began to take a stand on the issue. Some losing their businesses for the stand they made. Same sex marriage became the issue, again pastors all over the country began to search church constitutions and by-laws for ways to survive if they refused to marry people of the same gender. The Supreme Court settled the problem for them by making the marriage legal, so the church is out and no longer needed in the matter. The victory was settled and celebrated with the Whitehouse decked out in the rainbow colors.

---

[2] Note: Rationalization means to find plausible but untrue reasons for conduct. Webster's New Explorer Dictionary (Merriam-Webster, Inc. 1999) 433

Well, the battle still rages on for the soul of this nation [it seems we cannot see the forest for the trees], at the very beginning of the coronavirus pandemic one of the first decisions made was to *declare the church "non-essential."* God's representatives and the Word of God had no part with science and facts in the decision-making. Secular society has won a silent battle – as the church obeyed without question. Isn't it amazing how easy without fanfare the church was closed down and God's spokespersons went home to be led by secular leaders who after eight months still have not given God, our Creator, a favorable public mention? The God of Abraham, Isaac, and Jacob even though many of them claim to be Christians.

Meanwhile, in Los Angeles the battle still rages on between city officials and the local church – one newscaster reported that Pastor John MacArthur has been open throughout the pandemic and faces many uphill court battles as a result. We should pray for him and others who refused to bow to man! Churches in Las Vegas were restricted to 10 or less for any services or meetings, while the Casinos were limited to 50% of capacity. It was reported that one pastor rented space and held his services in the casino and still has to appear in court for violation of (?) code. Other pastors had to contend with the city officials shutting off their water and electricity. Pastors, and politics cannot settle God's business in the flesh. The president, the governor nor the mayor are called to speak for God. I cried and I am sure you did as loved ones had to struggle with the lost of fathers, mothers, children, and grandparents who were simply assigned a number and buried. When chaplains on duty had to minister through plate-glass windows. The church again was told by the secular society not more than ten and that outside [rain or shine]. Did you serve communion during the church closing? What will be new when you return to services in the sanctuary? With each attempt by the prince of this world to silence or neutralize the local church and Christianity he seems to gain a little more ground with society. There are always casualties in battle, in Vietnam, when sure death was sprayed in the form of nerve gas [blowing in the uncontrollable wind] we did not retreat back to the safety of the base camp [the 5th wire] – we lost some but stayed in the battle and seized the objective. Some leaders abandoned their churches and other facilities and now after nearly a year they are finding themselves fighting mold and mildew. Some did not communicate with their membership and has found out that some have died, and others have moved on. We are admonished to fail not to assemble ourselves together as we look for the coming of Christ [see Hebrews 10:25].

Those local churches and individual Christians who adhere to the truth of God's Word and daily prayerfully search the Scriptures will find themselves vulnerable to the wiles and temptations of the devil. Still, the old adage "it must be right, because everybody is doing it," is creating a toxic worldly society even impacting many persons in the local churches today who are willfully ignorant of his devices. Sadly, biblical doctrine [teaching] is not a priority for many today. Therefore, secular culture easily leaves its imprint on the local church culture; and now that many churches have divorced or rejected the Holy Spirit and the truth of God's Word with, "We do not want to frighten the people off!" Oh, but God is still working! With the COVID-19 pandemic, we are seeing *a spiritual hunger for the Word* like we have never seen before. If there was ever a time when the churches need the New Testament apostolic ministries [functions] – the time is now! And even more so when the virus is gone. In times like these, it is much easier for false prophets and false teachers to penetrate and operate undetected spreading ungodly institutional religion with its entertainment(ism). Though the Word of God promises that, "In the last days it shall be," says God, "that I will pour out My Spirit on all flesh; your sons and your daughters shall prophesy, your young men shall see visions, and your old men shall dream dreams. Even on My menservants and maidservants I will pour out My Spirit in those days, and they shall prophesy" (Acts 2:17-18).

Certainly, this prophesy is being fulfilled; we see the signs around the world that the Spirit is really here penetrating the darkness of this world through apostolic functions (see Ephesians 4:11). This is not necessarily a denominational or non-denominational matter as both are reaching spiritual ineffectiveness. Not far from our home in Fayetteville, sits an exceptionally large church building with a "For Sale" sign out front. In fact, after I checked, there are within several miles of our home there are three other such church buildings, one is a Mega-church building. God wants to use local churches that are Christ-centered and Bible-believing wherein the five *apostolic functions* of Ephesians 4:11 can thrive! In the world a person who goes around claiming to be something they are not, when they are found out to be a phony, they are immediately called to account, but in the church, there is truly little accountability. These issues will be developed more fully in chapters 9-10.

Another threat to Christianity is rationalism, this ungodly faction long ago realized that controlling what young people are taught, or not taught will ultimately determine the moral and philosophical standards of future generations. This deception is happening across our entire nation – in plain sight! Statistically, the rate of moral decay has more acceleration in this present generation than all previous generations combined. Even our government leaders have passed bills that has in the name of economic growth endorsed this moral decay. The updated secular moral code today says,

---

"If you can get away with it, it's alright."

We have been duped! Considering the fact that the United States became the world's greatest superpower and as stated earlier, the depository of Christianity, [America has been blessed with more Bible colleges, seminaries, churches, Christian bookstores, Christian television and radio stations than all the rest of the world combined].

However, God has never allowed any nation to hold to sin to the degree that we see in America today and remain excluded from judgment. This is especially true when the people have access to the truth of God's Word made available to them as we have (see Romans 1:1-21). The Bible warns that we [all the people] will be held accountable for the grace, resources and opportunities God has given us (see Luke 12:48).

One of the greatest tragedies of all is that much of the African American local church of the twenty-first century has capitulated. This means as African Americans, we cannot afford to continue to live as though we will not have to pay a price for our sins and resulting consequences. Atrocities of the past that our fore parents experienced under slavery, Jim Crow, the hatred of racism and the trauma of white supremacy and white privilege have been passed on through the genes to subsequent generations until this day.[3] They turned to God! God is able! We need to turn back to Him! He is our only hope! During the Great Awakening revivals in the south, the Baptist and Methodist preachers did not have the education of the Anglican Church and appealed to the poor and illiterate. Most slaves were never taught the faith [the whole

---

[3] Jay R. Leach, *We Would See Jesus* (Trafford Publishing 2020) 117

counsel of God] as the ministers' "fiery" sermons put the emphasis on "emotions" as the sign of conversion. Sadly, in many quarters [though unspoken] "emotions" continue to be the indicator in some churches for salvation to this day. However, the sermons gave the repressed slaves hope of escape from their earthly woes.[4] After the Civil War and the Emancipation, many African Americans turned their backs on God. Two of the prerequisites for the preacher in the slaves' invisible church were to know something about the Bible and be able to sing. Although that may have been adequate then, under the circumstances, sadly many African American churches still settle for that. Priority on "teaching them to *obey* all that I have commanded" (see Matthew 28:18) in many churches have absolutely nothing in place to help develop this intended "deeper life [to spiritual maturity]. Effective discipleship and evangelism strategies are non-existent in many of our Black local churches today.

There is no transformation without information!

After World Wars I and II, many local Black Churches placed *less and less emphasis* on *salvation* and the life beyond – but we are increasingly directing our activities toward the *economic, social,* and *political problems* of African Americans in the world.

As Christians we must always remember that our *allegiance* is *first* to God! [God-centered] (see Matthew 6:33; 2 Chronicles 7:14). In many such churches today, a "bloodless" institutional religion is practiced, and we often hear such postmodern clichés as, "whatever" and "it works for me/us." Though ignored by many, God's Moral Law is not optional and definitely not obsolete. Voluntary ignorance is no excuse. Even God's own people, Israel, did not get by as we shall soon see.

Like the sons of Issachar, we must be able to discern the urgency of the times![5] For the sake of the Christian church, our children, our grands and great grands, we must do all we can to make sure they chose to serve the Lord. Sadly, Satan has been able to effectively distort and progressively undermine our Christian values with each generation a little weaker than the preceding. The Scripture says, *"My people perish for a lack of [biblical] knowledge"* [bracket is mine]. We do well to stop, take

---

[4]   Ibid. page 108

[5]   1 Chronicles 12:32 "NKJV."

inventory, and learn from what happened in Noah's day – then take appropriate action!

Again, many African Americans are living without a true relationship with Jesus Christ, as more and more churches locked in traditions move from spiritual to non-spiritual institutional conduct, entertainment, clubs, and bloodless religion. A look into the Scriptures reveals that there will undoubtedly come a day when God will no longer be sympathetic to the cries of America or any other nation that has turned their back on Him. Listen to the prophet Jeremiah concerning the matter. Then the LORD said to me,

> *"Even if Moses and Samuel stood before Me,*
> *My mind would not be favorable toward this people.*
> *Cast them out of My sight and let them go forth"* (Jerimiah 15:1).

The very same concept is again expressed in Ezekiel 14:12-14: *"The word of the LORD came again to me saying: "son of man, when a land sins against Me by persistent unfaithfulness, I will stretch out My hand against it; I will cut off its supply of bread, send Famine on it, and cut off man and beast from it. Even if these three men, Noah, Daniel, and Job, were in it, they would deliver only themselves by their righteousness," says the Lord GOD.* Emphasis added.

The Scriptures above would have us to understand that another person's righteousness cannot save you. Like Israel, we cannot blame our families, the church or the leadership of the nation for the choices we make. Therefore, Godly living requires personal responsibility before the Lord. Receive the righteousness of God in Christ Jesus! As we travel throughout the region many African Americans are losing their homes, because of the depressed job market, prejudices, and lack of preparation – preparation includes first of all a right relationship with the Lord. When we were growing up, Sunday school was exciting even into the teen years. The Sunday school was a department with a strong prepared staff. The old rule of thumb said, the morning worship crowd would be equal to about one half the number in the Sunday school crowd. Today many of our churches have the 11 a.m. services, but Sunday School is nonexistent due to a lack of children and young adults. Many of the older adults show up for traditions sake.

I have heard many pastors brag about their ex-official status of all of the auxiliaries in the church – and the church suffered because over time the pastor becomes the one for all decisions etc. Neither a pastor alone nor the building alone are New Testament standards.

One blessing for the local Black church from the pandemic should be "vision" (where are we going? What is God's purpose for our existence?) In a nutshell most churches were frustrated when the churches were closed-down, because their total operation was shut-down. All that they did as a church was done inside of that building therefore, everybody went home. Let me tell you, 10 people can do some great Spirit-guided inventories and strategizing for reform, because we all know the church, we left because of the pandemic is gone forever! God has the right to change His Church as He sees fit. We better get innovation-minded and pray for wisdom and guidance for a spiritual existence within the New Testament standards. A year of programs and anniversaries does not substitute for the Great Commission. The world needs us. Jesus commanded, "Go!"(see Matthew 28:18-20).

What Satan cannot conquer? – He Contaminate!

Though a formidable foe, I am sure Satan found his true limitations while instigating the rebellion among the angels, which resulted in him being kicked out of heaven. Looking at his evil deeds and deceptions down through the ages may lead Satan and even some carnal Christians to believe that he still might have a chance to rule. However, the cross and the resurrection of Jesus Christ should have choked any of his dreams of taking the seat of the Most High God.

Now, knowing that his time is short, Satan has set a course to deceive, distort, destroy and what he cannot destroy he contaminates in future generations through what he accomplishes today. Because Paul does not want Satan to trick the church, he exhorts her to take a certain action!

The Call of the whole Body of Christ

Paul specifically defines the nature of the essential ministry of the Word that is the calling of *every* member of the body of Christ. In Colossians 3:15-17, notice his Spirit-guided counsel:

11

"And let the peace of God rule in your hearts, to which also you were called in one body: and be thankful. Let the word of Christ dwell in you richly in all wisdom, teaching and admonishing one another in psalms and hymns, and spiritual songs, singing with grace in your hearts to the Lord. And whatever you do in word or deed, do all in the name of the Lord Jesus, giving thanks to God the Father through Him."

Paul visualizes a well-prepared body of Christ with the Word of God dwelling in their hearts – alert and positioned to do what God has designed the *whole* body of Christ to do. Do what? Again, Paul is sharply specific: **teaching** and **admonishing**. He is proposing that every believer is designated to have a teaching, as well as praying and giving ministry. Amen! This "ministry of all believers" is an "all of God's people all of the time" mission. What is this saying? It is unhealthy for any church today if, the pastor is the only teacher.

Therefore, no matter where God has placed the teacher in the body of Christ – he or she needs to be taught the kingdom, and everyone being taught need also to teach and reproduce themselves. Being a pastor, I know that the pastor needs to be surrounded by well-trained teachers and faithful, loving admonishers. This may seem radical to some pastors, but Christ the Chief Shepherd, is the only Head of the body, the Church. Therefore, the pastor as under shepherd is a member in the body of Christ right along with all the other members.

Many institutional churches due to their secular organizational aspects assume that because of the pastor's gifts and a certain level of maturity has been noticed, and because he or she is now a biblical scholar trained for the pastorate, spiritually healthy – is able to live [*in isolation?*] without the normal protections and encouragements that they would want for *any* other member.

So, functional pastoral isolation is often instantly set up upon their arrival. The NIV lists some fifty statements that I call "one another ministries," which call us to a special kind of life together – for *all* in the body.

'In fact, The New Testament puts much emphasis on the need for all Christians including pastors and other leaders to know one another closely and intimately enough to be able to bear one another's burdens, confess faults to one another, encourage, exhort, and admonish one another – to minister to one another with the Word, song, and prayer.

Many of today's local churches have managed to do away with the true a apostolic model of New Testament ministry and have completely reduced the church's witness to proclaim and promote an institutional program. In so doing, the churches have removed the major safeguards of prayer meetings, Bible teaching, and admonition for the health of the churches' spirituality and growth to maturity within. Therefore, these losses have greatly weakened the effectiveness in the eyes of the world outside. Many dying churches today follow this same pattern.

Others turn to the blame game railing against the government, schools, humanism, and the local apathetic culture. Our very life depends on a daily diet of the Word of God. A priest was noted for admonishing the people, *"preach, preach and sometimes use words."* [6]

The real culprit in this cultural expulsion of God, Christ, and the Holy Spirit with His gifts and ministries, is the local church herself. Although we feed from the buffet of truth with our family and friends once a week – we have remained silent and uninvolved in the lives of our co-workers in the marketplace, the lost, our family members, friends and neighbors. Does our "daily walk" agree with our "daily talk?"

The reason most people today know so little of God is because the Christians they know have developed amnesia when it comes to communicating Jesus to them through righteous living. This silence advances the devil's agenda to kill *truth anywhere he finds it.* Thus, in John 8:44, Jesus describes the devil as both a liar and a murderer. Let us get with it! Jesus said it and that settles it. He says,

> *"He was a murderer from the beginning, and does not stand in truth, because there is no truth in him. When he speaks a lie, he speaks from his own [resources], for he is a liar and the father of it."*

Voluntary spiritual and biblical ignorance have changed the way some Christians speak of the devil. In some cases, they speak as if he is above God. Others in their worldly enlightenment do not believe the devil or his demons exist. But Scripture assures us that Christ defeated him on Calvary according to the promise (carefully study Genesis 3:15). And on several occasions, when it looked as if Satan had won for example, at the death of Abel, the good seed was cut off (see Genesis 4).

---

[6]   Francis of Assisi 1225 A.D.

Again, he no doubt gloated when Jesus died on the cross. God always has the last word!

The devil is not omnipresent nor all-knowing like God, but he has many demons to do his bidding. Demons are spirits also, as we see in the Gospels when Jesus cast them out of people. They do not have bodies, but their presence can be sensed. And many of us have had times when we sensed their very evil presence sometimes even in the church building itself during a worship service or other activities.

What about us?

Much is written and preached about the death of Christianity in many European countries where young people especially students have never heard of God or Jesus and have no concept of who or what He is. When this is aired here in America we hear, "Shame on them, how could they let that happen?" Surprisingly the same is true for the most part here in this present generation among our own teens and young adults.

Many churches have a fair showing when it comes to youth and young adult ministries, but most do not! Even among those who have grown up in church and regularly attended youth ministries and Sunday school, yet many have no real knowledge of Jesus Christ or the Bible. Much of the sermons today are clichés 20 to 40 minutes about prosperity and pep talks on how to get more stuff. Jesus is used as a great example, because He helped the poor.

Some pastors seldom if ever speak any longer about sin, repentance, or the blood of Jesus, but he or she gets applauded for such an inspiring, but never challenging message.

In other churches basic Bible knowledge is missing or so meshed with societal and cultural values that true biblical redemption in Jesus Christ has become obscure! This is so obvious in the way local churches have turned to entertainment(ism) as they strive to survive today after having neglected or simply thrown away a generation of youth and young adults.

It is obvious that God's moral law is no longer the norm – along with the rejection of the standards of biblical marriage and the family. Biblical "teaching" and "admonishing" remains God's way! A handshake will never replace the necessary "born again" from above experience of John 3:3.

"By grace you are saved through faith, and that not of yourselves, it is the gift of God" (Ephesians 2:8).

In many cases, such truth is twisted and watered down simply to "believe" [believe in belief]? Satan has wasted no time filling the void with false prophets (teachers), sowing syntheses of misunderstood facts, partial truths, and even straight out lies about Jesus Christ and salvation. At the same time, such people have little or no knowledge of Christianity, and the true way to get to heaven.

Social media is their Bible. And their god is usually a blend of philosophies and faith, along with their own personal view of morality when it comes to truth and life. And with that, the world and many in the church continue daily down the slippery slope unaware or ignoring a global storm on the horizon, held back by the Holy Spirit working through His people, the true body of Christ!

CHAPTER TWO

JUST AS IF I HAVE NEVER SINNED
[J U S T I F I C A T I O N]

But the free gift is not like the offense. For if by the one man's offense many died, much more the grace of God and the gift by the grace of the one Man, Jesus Christ, abound to many (Romans 5:15).

Week after week we hear many sermons on television, radio, internet, other social means, and in the churches, but few of them speak plainly of the dark condition of the unsaved souls and the solution, which is found in the death, burial, and resurrection of Jesus Christ [the gospel] (1 Corinthians 15:1-5).

Such neglect of the gospel is the cause for increasing numbers of people dying daily having never heard of Christ and His blood shed on behalf of humanity. We are saved by grace through faith, and not of ourselves; it is the gift of God. However, I do not believe there has ever been a genuine conversion yet, that was not preceded by *godly fear* and *repentance*. Since godly fear and repentance are biblical and objective prerequisites – they are not subject to private interpretation!

The Word of God is always objective, and there are those in every generation who strive to make it subjective. God's Word like God Himself is immutable, unchanging. Being world travelers, my wife and I have noticed that people in one location of the world may *justify* something that a group at another location call taboo, the same holds true here in different areas of the United States. That is all the more reason Christians must prayerfully search the Scriptures for truth themselves daily under the guidance of the Holy Spirit. Sadly, many strive to *justify* their thoughts, behavior, and actions in reference to the truth of God's Word the same way but, subjectively.

Paul explains as stated earlier, man did not begin with ignorance and work his way up to intelligence as explained by the evolutionist. Instead, he began with a brilliant revelation of the power and wisdom of God – but turned his back on it. Man knows there is something wrong with him (Romans 3:23).

God had revealed Himself in the things seen in the very created world; so, everyone should see evidence of God's existence and power. As a result, people who have never heard the Gospel are still without excuse. Vain thinking and foolish reasoning [rationalization] have turned people from the truth to lies (study carefully Romans 1:19-21):

- Many of the elite and intellectuals today turn to Greek, Roman and other philosophers – even pop psychology, honoring their words above the Word of God.
- They turn downward to idolatry which is running rampart to honor the creature (flesh) rather than the Creator.

They began with a clear knowledge of God and His judgment against sin. In spite of their knowledge of God, they still choose to worship self instead of God (review God's reaction to such rebellious behavior in the 14th and 15th chapters of the Book of Jeremiah). Then when troubles come upon them, "O God help me!" This religious mockery today which has substituted a handshake for repentance tend to forget that Jesus clearly taught, *"Except you repent, you shall likewise perish"* (Luke 13:3,5).

The Gospel of God

In the very first chapter and first verse we see the theme of the entire Book of Romans namely, [the Gospel of God]. The Gospel of God is the largest possible designation of the whole body of *redeeming truth!* The God that Paul magnifies in this Epistle is:

- Not a respecter of persons (Romans 2:11).
- Not the God of the Jews only, but He is also the God of the Gentiles. (Romans 3:29).
- Not the God of all so, clearly all the world is found guilty before Him. (Romans 3:19).

God's Remedy: The Doctrine of Justification

He has a righteousness available for us if we accept it; otherwise, man is destined for destruction and without God it is an impossible condition that man cannot fix. How can God justify a sinner and remain righteous? How many times have we found our children guilty and deserving punishment, but we have shielded punishment because we loved them? How can God justify our guilt and remain righteous? How could He save sinful man whom He loved?

A president or governor can pardon a prisoner, but they cannot wipe the individual's slate clean – that person is still guilty, even though he or she has been pardoned. God found a way to pardon and also declare a person righteous. <u>God only, can justify or declare a person righteous.</u> Therefore, a redemption as vast as the great *need* must be provided and revealed. God provided a way known as justification.

He acquits the gospel believer of the divine verdict of condemnation and declares him or her to be righteous, for He has made it so (see Romans 3:24; 4:25; 5:1, 9, 18; 8:30; 1 Cor. 6:11).

In this dark world today, Satan is trying to minimize or counter the churches' efforts to meet this great need by deploying many false teachers, false religions, false theologies, and false worship forms. Yet, through this satanic maze of deception, the Scriptures clearly reveal that this *redemption* must be provided: **1)** It is the *only* way out for *all* humanity and **2)** It is in a manner that all humanity can meet – *simple childlike faith!*

Paul shows us that the completion of God's comprehensive promises to Abraham can never be made a reality until the completion of the bride of Christ, the true Church, is a reality and caught up to meet Jesus, the Bridegroom, in the air. The key phrase in this passage is "the righteousness of God (Romans 1:17, 3:21, 22).

THERE IS NO TRUE RIGHTEOUSNESS APART FROM THE RIGHTEOUSNESS OF GOD IN CHRIST JESUS!

We clearly see that justification is through the righteousness of God as set forth in the gospel as the *only remedy* for sin and human guilt toward God – by faith. In his letter to the Romans, Paul clearly states, "all have sinned and come short of the glory of God" (3:23). Therefore no one has achieved that standard, no one has loved and worshiped the Lord as they should (carefully study 3:11 – 5:11). Jesus took our sins and gave us His righteousness and as we are crucified with Christ, we are resurrected to new life *in* Christ (2 Corinthians 5:21). Also, we walk as a new creation[7] in Christ day by day as the Spirit of God leads every true child of God. *"If anyone is not filled with the Holy Spirit, he or [she] is none of His"* (study carefully Romans 5:12 – 8:13).

Reconciled to God

Now that Christ's death and resurrection has satisfied God's righteous demands, God is now able to turn toward us. God has made all believers new creatures in Christ and participants as ministers of reconciliation [all of the church – all of the time]. He has committed to us all, the word of reconciliation. As stated in an earlier section, we who are reconciled to God have the privilege of telling all people that God wants to restore them to a relationship with Himself (Romans 5:8).

God could now change His relationship toward us because our sins have been imputed (reckoned) to Christ, instead of to us as God placed our sins on Him. When Christ our offering was examined, the results were:

---

[7] 2 Corinthians 5:17

- In Him was no sin (1 John 3:5).
- He knew no sin (2 Corinthians 5:21).
- He did not sin (1 Peter 2:22).
- He was without sin (Hebrews 4:15).

His death was in our place and for our sins. As we believe in Jesus, God counts Jesus' righteousness as *our* righteousness. Jesus never sinned. Yet He died for our sins, so that we could be declared righteous, that is to say, *justified.* (v. 19) Praise God! That is the Good News that everyone needs to hear!

I believe in my heart that even in this evil day that those desiring to see and experience this great truth can do so. Jesus Christ did on the cross [in a body like yours and mine] what we could never do for ourselves. Praise God! He did for us what the Law could never do. *He took our place!* And when we accept Him by faith – God looks upon us:

- as being just as just as Jesus is just,
- as being just as righteous as Jesus is righteous,
- as being just as holy as Jesus is holy

In this day of denial and rejection of the truth of God's Word, we can be grateful to personally know that we are washed in the blood of Jesus Christ and hid with Him in God. Therefore, God does not see our old sinful nature, but He sees the blood of Jesus that covers us and the new divine nature which He has imparted to us.

As multiculturalism, universalism, humanism, atheism, materialism, and other beliefs encroach upon our local cultures denying the moral state of fallen humanity, we know that the fallen state is clearly described in the Word of God. We know the truth! Please prayerfully study: Genesis 6:5; I Kings 8:46; Psalm 14:1-3; Jeremiah 17:9; Mark 7:20-23; Romans 1:21-32; 3:9-19; I Corinthians 2:14; Galatians 5:19-21; Ephesians 2:1-3; and Colossians 1:21.

Deliverance made clear

The Scripture makes clear the fact, that the law was our schoolmaster to bring us to Christ for salvation, and now justified by grace through faith; we are no longer under the schoolmaster (Galatians

3:10-25). The just shall live by faith! [not by the Law, but by grace through faith]. Because of the grace of God, whoever ends up in hell, will be there by their own choice – it will not be because of Adam's transgression. If we just receive Christ, God will do the rest,

> *And the gift is not like that which came through the one who sinned. For the judgment which came from one offense resulted in condemnation, but the free gift which came from many offenses resulted in justification. For if by the one man's offense death reigned through the one, much more those who receive abundance of grace and of the gift of righteousness will reign in life through the One, Jesus Christ. Therefore, as through one man's offense judgment came to all men, resulting in condemnation even so through one Man's righteous act the free gift came to all men, resulting in justification of life* (Romans 5:16-18).

The truth of these tremendous verses is simply that: God's *free Gift namely grace, His only begotten Son the Lord Jesus Christ, without measure* outweighs the transgression of man! Through Adam came death – and yes, .,. through Jesus Christ came grace and eternal life. Praise God!

All who will come to God through Christ Jesus –
will be made righteous through His shed blood.

The grace that saves us teaches that, we were *by nature* the children of the devil, translated out of the kingdom of darkness *"into the kingdom of His dear Son or kingdom of light"* (Colossians 1:13).

Have we been duped?

Because of voluntary biblical and spiritual ignorance, many in the local churches today are listening to and trying to assimilate worldly values with the church cultural values in order to accommodate and be accepted. Some churches except unsaved people as bonifide members hoping they will one day be saved. Colossians 1:12 ends with *"the inheritance of the saints in the light."* As I stated in an earlier section, prophetic

Scriptures warn us that in the Last Days deceiving and seducing spirits will turn *many away* because of abounding sin.

Research shows that it is obvious the ways of the world
have had a lot more influence on Christians than we
have had on the world during this last generation.

Satan has sent these *"deceiving spirits"* into the local Christian communities today trying to fool God's people <u>to trade a biblical truth for a worldly standard</u>. We are constantly being tempted by his major deceptions today coming from the *influences* of our secular society gone wild. They try to make the difference between black and white a gray area, and the same [between true and false]. The following prophetic Scriptures warn that many will turn because of abounding sin (study carefully, Matthew 24:11, 24; 1 Timothy 4:1; 2 Timothy 3:1-5, 13-14, 16-17).

Are you concerned that there has never been a
society where moral values have deteriorated so
fast and drastically, in such a short period of time
as America has over the past 50 or 60 years?

Secularism is one of Satan's most dangerous deceptive attacks against Christianity. [<u>Secularism is the substitution of worldly values for Christian standards and values as set forth in the Word of God</u>]. Like secularism, humanism, another of Satan's deceptions is characterized by replacing biblical Christian standards with worldly standards. Both are evidenced by attitudes and lifestyles. Satan has used humanism to affect and promote his humanistic philosophies in textbooks at all levels of education in this country.

Many are the ideas about God and who He really is, gives rise to a god created by our own imagination. Often, we hear someone say, "My God and I." If Christ is not God who is? Well, many will tell what they think about that, but only the Bible tells us distinctly who God is:

- The Bible explains, not only who God is, but also how much He loves us and that He created us for His glory.
- The Bible explains how man rebelled for independence when God gave them a choice or freewill.
- The Bible explains how sin began in the angelic realm by an angel named Lucifer, and entered the human realm, when the fallen angel [now Satan/ the devil] deceived man through the serpent to renounce God, thus making a wrong choice in the Garden of Eden.
- Man fell alienating himself from God – and subjecting all humankind to the bondage of sin (Genesis 1-3).
- The Bible explains God's prophetic message of deliverance from the very foundation of the world (Genesis 3:15).
- The Bible explains that God was in Christ reconciling the [lost] world unto Himself.
- The Bible explains that God gave His only begotten Son to accomplish the mission by shedding His blood on the cross, our sacrifice for sin.
- The Bible establishes the fact that Christ through His death and resurrection is the only way for humankind to get eternal life and on to the Father's house [heaven].
- The Bible is God's answer book to His children, He urges us to prayerfully study it, meditate on it, and gain understanding through the Holy Spirit, our Teacher.
- The Bible is the Word of God – and it has been said that the Word of God is shallow enough for a young child to wade in, yet deep enough to drown a full-grown man.

Heaven is a place of light. In Revelation 21 we are told that there is no need for sun or stars there – the Lamb is the light of the city. His radiance will furnish the light where the saints will live and move throughout eternity. Only saints will dwell there, who are clothed with purity, and perfection, God's holiness, and the righteousness of the Lord Jesus Christ (II Corinthians 5:21). We must have a personal relationship with Christ, our Savior and Lord to go to heaven. Do you know Him?

Natural man is incapable of enjoying the inheritance of light in this body. By nature, the natural person is darkness. His or her mind is darkened, with impure thoughts, and their hearts are desperately wicked and must be changed [this necessitates a "new birth" from above] before they can enter the kingdom of light, here – and at the end of life's journey (John 3:3; 1 John 1:7).

Imagine an unregenerate person entering heaven – heaven would then be hell. Heaven is a *prepared* place for a *prepared* people. It is the primary task of *every* pastor to prepare his or her people for the journey to get there! Think about it, no person in the *flesh* has ever obeyed God's command. What God commands, He provides and makes possible to the individual. Christ is made unto us wisdom, righteousness, sanctification, and redemption. Praise God! The message of the resurrection of Jesus changed the world in His day, and it still divides humankind into two groups:

- Those saved and in a right relationship with Christ.
- Those who are not saved, and therefore not in any relationship with Christ.

Rapture Ready

The resurrection of Jesus Christ teaches us that death is not the end. Death is an enemy; but to the believer, death is an exit from a life of sorrow into a life of peace and joy in the presence of Jesus, the One who conquered death. The resurrection of Jesus Christ is the secret of the New Testament message. One day, suddenly, "in the twinkling of an eye" we will be caught up (raptured) from pain and heartaches to eternal joy. We will be translated from this world of sorrow to a world of singing, praising, and jubilant hallelujahs! We need to emphasize that this not so for the unsaved. In spite of what Hollywood is saying. "Except you are born again from above this does not include you" (see John 3:3).

Heaven begins here on earth; however, we just get a taste because we are still in our human body. But the *fulness* of our inheritance will be realized after the rapture of the saints, when we are removed out of this dark world into the perfect day where there is no gloom, no misty fog – only the glory of God – the brilliance of light that only the face of Jesus can produce. O, reader, "are you rapture ready?"

Jesus said, *"Come unto me, all you who labor and are heavy laden, and I will give you rest"* (Matthew 11:28). We can shout the victory over death, hell, and the grave, because we believe in Him who conquered all of death, hell, and the grave.

Certainly, the line is clearly drawn by the truth of God's Word, that His redeeming love, and His indescribable power, has translated us out of the kingdom of darkness and into the Kingdom of His dear Son.

The Church in the darkness of this wicked world

We hear much negative talk about the church and church culture today. We hear such comments as: they are just another country club or its antiquated and need to be updated. Then there are those who think of the church as just another political action committee. In spite of all her weaknesses, hypocrisies, and sin; the church is the most powerful force on earth for good – from its earliest existence until now. It has been a light and paradox in the darkness of this world.

God created and designed the church to be so. In the paradox, we wonder how can a church reflect both *sin* and *darkness* and at the same time reflect *light* and *righteousness?* How can it be the agent of both *spiritual ignorance* and *spiritual revelation knowledge?* So, we find the natural and the spiritual in the church together.

The natural and the spiritual

In Matthew 13, Jesus uses parables to describe the conditions in the world during the period between His First and Second Coming. One parable is called, the parable of the wheat and the tares. In the parable, Jesus Himself, the Son of Man plants wheat in the field of the world. The wheat [good seed] called the *"children of the kingdom,"* believers. However, once the wheat is planted the devil comes in and plants tares. The tares look like wheat but produces no grain.

The tares represent *counterfeit Christians,* whom Jesus called, *"the sons of the evil one."* Outwardly, like tares to wheat the counterfeit Christians look real. The wheat and tares grow up together and for a while look just alike. One day the workers noticed the tares growing among the wheat and ask if they should dig them up. The Lord answers, "No." Uprooting the tares would destroy the wheat. Instead, He said, "Let the wheat and the tares grow together until the harvest" (Matthew 13:30).

Jesus concludes the parable; the harvest will take place at the close of the age when He will send His angels into the field to separate the tares from the wheat. The tares will be burned in the judgment, but the wheat will be gathered into the father's barns. True Christians, the sons of the kingdom, are those who have been born again. Jesus said, *"Except one is born again, he [or she] cannot see the kingdom of God"* (John 3:3). Emphasis added. Peter later describes the Christian's "born again experience as not of corruptible seed but incorruptible, through the living and abiding Word of God" (1 Peter 1:23). The "sons of the evil one" [false or counterfeit Christians] were never "born again" by the power of the Holy Spirit through faith in the finished work of Jesus Christ (1 Corinthians 1:1-5; Romans 1:16).

Wisdom from the past

Early Christians challenged the power of heathen kings and surrendered their life's blood to testify that they had complete, and unshakable faith in the Man Jesus Christ. His resurrection still speaks to every sinner on earth. If you believe Jesus died and rose again, and if you will confess with your mouth as you believe in your heart, then Christ will save you (see Romans 10:9, 10). Once saved you are translated into the kingdom of His dear Son. Does that sound like a place you want to be?

CHAPTER THREE

GROW IN GRACE AND THE KNOWLEDGE OF OUR LORD
[S A N C T I F I C A T I O N]

Grace and peace be multiplied to you in the knowledge of God and of Jesus our Lord, as His divine power has given to us all things that pertain to life and godliness, through the knowledge of Him who called us by glory and virtue, by which have given unto us exceedingly great and precious promises, that through these you may be partakers of the divine nature, having escaped the corruption that is in the world through lust (II Peter: 1-4).

But refuse profane and old wives' fables and exercise thyself rather unto godliness (1 Timothy 4:7)

Again, we were created for the glory of God. However, we saw earlier, that God's original design for mankind was rejected by Adam and Eve in the Garden of Eden. As descendants of Adam, we bore his likeness which had become a distortion of God's image. But as we walk in the

27

light of Christ, we are transformed into His likeness, the last Adam. What did the "first Adam" lose through *sin* that the "second Adam," Jesus Christ, desires to restore by His Spirit through you and me?

Holy unto the Lord

In my personal study of God's Word recently, I looked straight at a truth that I already knew, but rediscovered in an entirely new way? That happened as I studied Romans 12:1, it led me to the second step in the *one* salvation process; *a living sacrifice, holy, acceptable to God, which is your reasonable service.* In the first step of salvation, you personally and genuinely *heard* and *believed* that Jesus had shed his blood for your sins and only through His death and resurrection could you be saved – you received eternal life. Do not let anyone talk you out of that truth (see I Corinthians 15:1-4; Romans 10:9-10).

Now, here is the meat of the matter, the second step requires believers to *separate themselves [holy unto the Lord]*! Notice:

Salvation *comes only through the sacrifice of Christ –*
Holiness *comes only through the sacrifice of yourself to Christ.*

A Living Sacrifice

Many conversions today do not include the second step of holiness, which requires *each* of us and the individual convert alike, to present our body a "living sacrifice" to God. This step of holiness also requires a separation to the Lord – and remember, our body is the temple of the Holy Spirit.

Additionally, we must emphasize at this point, that this presenting is different from the decision to put our faith in Christ for salvation (*justification*). This second step sometimes is instantly activated the moment after a person is born again. However, the percentage of people in this category is exceedingly small.

I personally spent some time floundering around like a fish out of water before I really had a break-through with my personal holiness (*sanctification*). Sadly, many churches have tossed out this second mandatory step in salvation. Take a look at your local church, the

28

empty pews make it obvious – there is little or no "What then" taught about *life* after *believing?* Clarification and commitment are a must here! Without them the local church would be producing carnally what many unchurched and ungodly parents are producing physically, [wild rebels].

Sadly, much *present truth* is overlooked in the Christian community today. Several generations ago, much was taught by example, at home, the pastor's sermon, and Sunday school in the close-knit communities and neighborhoods many of us grew up in. However, that example is not as prominent today therefore, Holy Spirit-guided discipleship [training and action] is imperative more than ever today! How? Keep reading!

If an unsaved person seeks to present him or herself to the Lord as a living sacrifice the Lord cannot receive them – for the simple reason, their presentation can in *no way* be holy and acceptable to God. Perhaps you may be asking why? The Word of God has made it clear, the *only* acceptable approach to God is through the *shed blood of Jesus Christ.* "And without shedding of blood there is no remission [forgiveness] (Hebrews 9:22 also see Psalms 66:18).

Seeking to present yourself to God without belief in Jesus Christ is ludicrous. We hear of local churches that take people into membership before they have accepted Christ – claiming to be doing this hoping the individual will come to Christ at a later date. That person is brought along through some act of unbiblical personal sacrifice rather than through Christ's act of sacrifice. The Bible makes it clear, "Believe on the Lord Jesus Christ, and you will be saved" (Acts 16:31). Adding any other condition or way is not biblical.

It is clear in Romans 12:1 that Paul was addressing Christians who had been saved. He was urging a decision of their own freewill to dedicate themselves to a deeper and more meaningful Christian life. The Lord desires His children to present themselves to Him as living sacrifices.

Sin shall not have dominion

A fruitful spiritual life for many in our churches today, is similar to being on a treadmill jogging on an on but going nowhere in their Christian life. The concept of discipleship must be seen and pursued as a distinct truth from salvation. Discipleship is a bad word to many churches today. A disciple is more than a *leaner.* It takes a disciple to make a disciple. The key truth in this passage is presenting yourself as a living sacrifice. Listen to Paul, as he encourages the church at Rome to consecrate themselves, "I beseech you therefore, brethren, by the *mercies of God*, that you present your bodies a living sacrifice."

In view of all that Christ has done for those who are His, the only acceptable worship is to offer yourselves *completely* to the Lord. Under God's control, the believer's yet *unredeemed body* can and must be *yielded* to Him as an instrument of righteousness (Romans 6:12, 14).

While sin shall not have dominion over you [those in Christ]; yet sin must be able to exercise control in our bodies, otherwise the apostle Paul's admonition,

> *"And do not present your members as instruments of unrighteousness to sin but present yourselves to God as being alive from the dead, and your members as instruments of righteousness to God"* (v. 13).

But sin **does not** have to reign there, so Paul
expresses his confidence that those who are
Christ's **will not let it** – for they are **not**
under law but under grace (Romans 6:14).

The mortal body is the only remaining repository where sin finds the believer vulnerable. The brain and its thinking processes are a part of the body and therefore tempt our souls with its sinful lusts. Until our soul is yielded to the Holy Spirit's renewal – our body is a potential wreck waiting to happen!

The soul comprises our mind, affections (emotions), and our will. As born from above believers, our old self died with Christ, and the life we now enjoy is a new divinely given life – that is, the life of Christ Himself (see Galatians 2:20).

Now that we are removed from the unregenerate self's presence and control – we *should not* entertain the remaining memories of the old sinful ways as if we were still under their evil influences! Here is where the rubber meets the road! Remember, a dead sacrifice remains where you put it – but a living sacrifice can move about and is subject to crawl or jump off the altar. Often, we hear of those who made a serious commitment to Christ, but later move away or [backslide]. Most of our churches are not equipped to handle this crisis in people's lives and we lose many of them back to the world or they remain a *spiritual* casualty among us. The late Dr. Billy Graham concluded in his research that about 90% of American Christians were living defeated *spiritual* lives according to the Scriptures:

- We know what to say in Christian circles, but our actions or fruit are broadcasting our weakness to the standards set by our society.
- The picture we portray here indicates that many Christians are still bound by their old sinful nature.
- The cause is mainly deception just as Jesus warned us when He said,

"For false prophets (teachers) will appear and perform great signs and miracles to deceive even the elect if that were possible" (Matthew 24:24).

Remember, deception is determined by the results produced by one's actions when compared to the teachings of the Word of God. The church is losing ground daily to the overpowering ability of our society to develop through influence and teaching its own post-modern humanistic standards and worldly lifestyles.

Do not be conformed

In Romans 12:2, Paul admonishes, *"do not be conformed to this world, but be transformed by the renewing of your mind."* In a day when Christianity is being rejected for almost any belief that bears no responsibility, those who are Christ's should not assume any outward appearance that does not truly reflect what is really in their heart. Be real!

We are not to let the suggestions, ideas, beliefs, values, and contemporary thinking of this world, which are always dominated by Satan to deceive – conform our thinking – but we are admonished to renew our mind! (see also 2 Corinthians 4:4).

A renewed mind to the rescue

Paul admonishes that we *be transformed by the renewing of our minds.* The Greek word used here from which the English word *"metamorphosis"* comes, means a change in outward appearance. We learned about the word metamorphosis in primary school. When our teacher taught us how a worm would spin itself into a cocoon and sometime later emerges as a beautiful butterfly. In the Book of Matthew, the writer uses this same word to describe the Transfiguration of Christ (Matthew 17:2). Just as Christ briefly displayed outwardly:

- His inner divine nature and glory at the transfiguration.
- Christians should outwardly *manifest* their inner, *redeemed natures,* not once but [24/7] daily (see 2 Corinthians 3:18; Ephesians 5:18).

Whereas daily many of the Christian television shows tell us that the power is within each of us to "just do it." However, this is mostly told to a mixed multitude. Most do not distinguish whether what is said pertains to the saved only or both. Though we do not want to offend anyone, God's Word is clear. Please know, this kind of *transformation* or *renewing of the mind* can come *only* to those born again from above as the Holy Spirit enables us to change our thinking:

- Through our consistent study, meditation, memorization, and application of Scripture (Ps. 119:11).
- Through a renewed mind, which is one saturated with the Word of God and controlled by the Spirit of God through practical life application.
- Through holy living which glorifies God.
- Through a renewed mind – you may prove what is that good and acceptable and perfect will of God.
- Through a spiritual life that is morally and spiritually spotless – as compared to the OT sacrificial animals were to be (Lev. 22:19-25).

The reality we face

Today other terms such as inclusive and the new tolerance as taught and lived in the worldly society around us has now voided truth to much of the population and has destructively spilled over into the church culture. Of course, this inclusive and tolerance are only acceptable if you, the Christian conform [agree] with secular humanism's definition or meaning of the words, most of which defies God's Moral laws.

The biblical term "grace" [undeserved divine favor] is another of the most misunderstood, misused, and mis-defined terms in the Bible. In fact, there are those who falsely claim that grace abolishes the requirements for the standards of holiness above. As for as these people are concerned that is enough to seal their home in heaven – therefore materialism and hedonism become their focus and practice.

It may come as a shock to some, but much of the church is buying into this falsity. For example, some denominations have striped their church hymnals of all hymns that mention the blood of Jesus. By the same token other churches have discontinued the Lord's Supper (communion) because it is exclusive [to only those born again from above]. To deny the blood of Jesus [His death, burial, and resurrection] is to deny the only solution from sin to salvation (see I Corinthians 15:1-4).

Like a cancer, this satanic humanistic behavior is spreading throughout [denying the gospel truth]. In reality if not countered soon, repentance and the new birth will be lost – which would negate a life of holiness [separation] and even eternal life. Satan could care less if your church has five or five thousand members, so long as they yield to secularistic and hedonistic beliefs and live freely?

Today, much of the church has openly turned their back on the truth of God's Word, while others have simply turned their heads away or just overlook the pervading extreme permissiveness that has invaded. That way they exclaim, "I don't know what is going on." When this thinking is tolerated it produces personal gods, personal devils, personal morals, many counterfeit forms of godlessness allowed to operate openly in the church – mainly for fiscal and numerical purposes.

Many in the pews openly condone and defend such conduct and behavior as was demonstrated in the incestuous affair in the church at Corinth (see 1 Corinthians 5:1-8) wherein, the people prided their ability to be open-minded, inclusive, and resilient enough to tolerate or cope with it. Immorality is nasty business which if not countered results in the slippery slide into sin as described in (Romans 1).

The Gospel Truth

We dream and speak of heading toward a great future as prophesied by the media, science, gurus, politicians, and other natural input. The truth is the future is rushing toward us. We think the present makes sense only in light of the past. Therefore, much of the problem we face lie in our thinking. We humans write history looking though the rear-view mirror at where we have been. God creates history ahead of time. In other words, God never forecasts – He always back-casts. God creates history ahead of time. He *began* with the *end* in mind. The future is *always* incipient in the present.

Before the foundation of the world, the Lamb was slain!

Calvary was anticipated in God's breathe of life into Adam. The empty tomb confirmed the invasion of the future into the present. When Paul met the resurrected Jesus – he realized the future had been fast-forwarded into the present. That changed everything – it still does!

In my work, I talk with people in various denominational churches, Bible schools, and Para ministries who are increasingly voicing fundamental doubts concerning the survivability of the church. Please note, this criticism is not from people outside the church, but they are from people inside including pastors and other dedicated leaders who do like what they are experiencing in church. Not long ago I received a phone call from a young, frustrated pastor with a vision for the church he was called to pastor, he stated that after several months the old unanointed institutional religion (status quo) within the church was terribly upset with recommended changes. Their creed was the old adage – the seven last words of a dying church, "We have never done it like that!" His question was, "How do I resign?" The big problem in this case are people who cannot separate the *faith* from institutional *religion* or cannot picture a God larger than their ensuing experiences.

Many of these churches are folding today after the old wineskins have passed away – sadly, many times the new wineskins will not change due to customs and tradition. If this is your church, look for change in the coming future. If the Lord tarries many such churches will probably not survive after the COVID-19 pandemic. This condition is causing people to leave many of the local churches, not because they have lost the faith – but to preserve their faith! They insist that their church no longer contribute to their spiritual development.

Some claim that the church actually contributes to the rebellious attitude in their teenagers. This is a sad commentary repeated too often in many faith communities today. Over the centuries "the faith" in the hearts of man has been eroded intentionally by people and at the same time the value of life has also eroded, all orchestrated by the prince of this world I am sure.

Jude admonished the church two thousand years ago to, **contend for the faith that was _once_ entrusted to the saints.** (Jude 3). Jude's original purpose for writing this letter was to expound on the doctrine of salvation no doubt consisting of sin, guilt, repentance, God's love and grace, the forgiveness of sin and the changed lifestyle that follows the new birth from above! However, he was compelled [by the Spirit] to write about **the faith,** which is the entire **body of truth** held by believers everywhere – the Gospel of God and all its implications. This truth was under attack and had to be defended *once for all and entrusted*[8] *to the saints.* Truth has finality and is not subject to change. Jude felt led to warn that certain immoral men among them were perverting the grace of God (vv. 4, 10, 12, 14, 19).

He urged the saints [then and now], to remember what the apostles of our Lord Jesus Christ foretold. They said to you, "In the last times there will be scoffers who *will follow their own ungodly desires."* These are the men who divide you, who follow mere natural instincts and *do not have the Spirit* (vv. 18, 19; also see 2 Peter 3:3). Jude wants us to know **these false teachers are here and they are at work!** He points out that the coming of these false teachers were prophesied by Peter (2 Peter 2:1; 3:3).

Romans 8:9 clearly declares, "A person who does not have the Spirit is *clearly not saved."* Why is it so hard for church leaders and teachers to grasp that biblical truth? Here is the answer to the question in the prior section. Many Christians are leaving the traditional and institutional

---

[8]   The truth, a trust, conferred to all saints with the responsibility to complete the work. (Webster's New Explorer Dictionary and Thesaurus copyright 1999) 916.

churches today because many of the churches have left the faith and divorced the Holy Spirit with His gifts and ministries. Certainly, we cannot develop spiritually without the Spirit. Many churches across America have aborted the *faith* and adopted an institutional *bloodless religion*.

"A person who does not have the Holy Spirit
is clearly not saved" (Romans 8:9).

During the 50's and 60's the worldly American culture decided to walk away from the biblical worldview, moral values, and establish their own ethical standards – and much of the church culture has followed suit, adopted, and assimilated customs, laws, forms, and entertainment, eventually conformed to their gods and open sinful lifestyles. On Wednesday, October 21, 2020, the Pope sanctioned same sex associations for inclusivity's sake. In spite of what the Word of God has to say on the subject. Sadly, the earliest casualties in this depletion of the faith were: expository preaching and teaching along with the old hymns of the church and the study of biblical systematic theology. As a result, the secular society through a humanistic agenda has easily ripped the biblical worldview and the righteous heart out of much of the church.

"It is time we stopped wringing our hands in fear
and began lifting our hearts in prayer." Jay Leach

I stated earlier a secular education and a practical liberal orientation [institutional religion] had to replace old Bible-driven curriculums which incorporated discipleship, disciplines, virtues and values. Secularists gradually accomplished their ungodly goals through emotions and feelings based on liberal theologies, philosophies, psychology, and other forms of "what works for me" methodology. The goal being to destroy the foundations of Christianity, the faith (see Jude 3).

Biblical truth and virtues do not get a favorable mention in today's postmodernism and so-called post Biblical and post Christian world view [as demonstrated so boldly by the media and other entities in today's COVID-19 crisis]. What has the American church gained out of all of this pandemic facing the world today? While the world is clamoring "fear or facts," many in the church are shouting back "fear or faith!"

Since we know that if the Lord tarries it is going to be a different world with changes much different than 9/11, perhaps, we can come out of this with a glorious new church to the glory of God. Put the answer this way, it is not openly spoken, but the church is considered and given *"non-essential status"* during the ongoing coronavirus pandemic. What happened to the church's constitutional rights to freedom of religion and freedom of assembly? I read that on March 30, one pastor Rodney Howard-Browne in Florida was charged with unlawful assembly and violating the county's stay-home order. The media played up the story, "crazy Pentecostal pastor" endangers the health of his church members by recklessly disregarding governmental edicts for nonessential gatherings of more than 10 people. Is this a prelude to the return to house churches? While science and so-called facts are king? Shame on us if we allow our local churches to return to the same old mundane that led us to this place! It has almost been a year and many Christians and local churches have not even understood the relevance and spiritual importance of this *season of grace*. Many are focusing on the wrong things or just hanging out in a spiritual stupor. God has always intended His Church to be the head and never the tail! The church should be leading the culture not following it. God's Church and this country has strayed so far from our first love – Jesus Christ. What can we do? Repent and return!

As pastors and church leaders we must examine ourselves to make sure that *we* are personally in the faith once entrusted to the saints! If you are planning to return to leading with [self-centered] institutional religion, worldly wisdom and [a "what works for me mentality"] then expect the worse results, however, with a much smaller group of people. If we humbly repent and biblically return to spiritual heart knowledge and godly wisdom from above – the Spirit of God can grow us up to be fruitful [in the faith] for the glory of God. If we let Him! Note the apostle Paul's prayer, *"I pray that … you will know … the riches of the glory of His [Jesus'] inheritance in the saints"* (Ephesians 1:18).

Return to the Book

Many Christians believe that with experience you do not need doctrine this may hold true with institutional bloodless religion and man produced doctrine – but biblical doctrine works hand in hand with experience. Bible doctrine is truth. The more you know the Bible, the more you will know God. The more you know God, the more truth you will know – and the more you will be taught, rebuked, chastened, and trained. Jesus *promised, "But when he the Spirit is come, he will guide you into all truth* (John 16:13). The more you know God the more you will experience His *love* and His *will* – His will for us is that we walk filled with the Spirit with His Son and be like Him. The Bible is the ultimate source. Listen to the inspired writers,

> *All Scripture is given by inspiration of God, and is profitable for doctrine, for reproof, for correction, for instruction in righteousness, that the man of God may be complete, thoroughly equipped for every good work* (2 Timothy 3:16-17).

> *For the word of God is living and powerful, and sharper than any two-edged sword, piercing even to the division of soul and spirit, and of joints and marrow, and is a discerner of the thoughts and intents of the heart* (Hebrews 4:12).

The Word of God is comforting and nourishing to those who believe it and feed on it daily. It is also a tool of judgment and persecution for those who have not committed themselves to Jesus Christ. Some of the Hebrews born in the land were merely going through the motion of being Christians. God's Word exposed their shallow beliefs and false intentions and – God's Word is still exposing sin and deception today. These same sinful deficiencies have spread throughout the local faith communities today.

However, in all probability these shallow conditions are the tragic results of a decision much of the American church made some forty or sixty years ago to move several of the Lord's Kingdom operational commitments to include the Great Commandment (see Matthew 22:37-40) and the Great Commission (see Matthew 28:19-20) to voluntary or optional status? That is intentional disobedience. In fact, empty pews, worldliness, and wandering Christians hungry for spiritual food can be attributed to the absence of dedicated disciplines, and discipleship training in much of the American Church today. Combined, these two passages give us the primary objectives for the church *until* Christ returns to take His church out of this world.

Our ultimate Example

Some churches believe becoming like Jesus is impossible [more on this later]. We know that He is God; but we learned that He chose not to use His divinity for the very purpose of showing us by example – how to live a life of total dependency under the will of God the Father by the power of the Holy Spirit. While He never stopped being God – He became fully human. He used the same resources He has made available to all of us. We must look to our ultimate example, Jesus Christ, for what it looks like to walk with God:

- He is not only our Savior, and our Lord, but He is also our example.
- He walked and worked in the Spirit to show us <u>that we could do the same.</u>
- He displayed the fruit of the Spirit.
- He operated in the Spiritual gifts.
- He is what it looks like to be a fully devoted disciple of God.

Be wise and beware

- Again, I cannot overemphasize, "beware of churches that deny the Holy Spirit and His gifts and ministries!"
- Beware of churches that no longer make disciples and just urge people to just tithe and be good Christians.
- Beware of churches that are not Christ and Bible centered.

Outward appearance is not enough

Some churches have settled for an institutional religion [Cain], over the "true blood-washed faith that was once delivered to the saints" [Abel]. The Scripture characterizes such churches as, *"Having a form of godliness, but denying the power"* (2 Timothy 3:5). Paul exhorted Timothy to continue in the gospel of Jesus Christ in the face of a great increase of evil. We are in the last days, which comprise the time from Jesus' first coming until His Second Coming (study prayerfully Acts 2:17; 1 Timothy 4:1; Hebrews 1:1,2; 1 Peter 1;20; 1 John 2:18).

The Bible has absolute authority over our lives – based solely in our conviction that it does not merely contain the Word of God, but it is the Word of God in all of its parts (1 Timothy 3:16). In the last days, people will be characterized by various kinds of self-centeredness and unnatural perversions. Some will maintain an outward pretense speaking the vocabulary of Christianity but refusing the reality that the true Christian faith expresses (v. 5).

The power they deny is the very heart of the gospel of Christ:

- The resurrection of Jesus Christ
- The truth of the inspired Word of God
- The indwelling and overflowing of the Holy Spirit working within believers transforming their lives

We have the same Holy Spirit that led Jesus Christ to the cross and raised Him from dead, and we also have the Word of God, therefore, the local church can be humbly brought from mere institutional existence – to the faith once delivered to the saints.

Devote yourself to the Word of God, Spirit-filled living, Spirit-inspired devotion and bearing the fruit of the Spirit. Both the Spirit and the Word work hand in hand in through us to keep us Christ and Bible-centered in word and deed.

Do not be fooled by religiosity

Does Jesus' Spirit-filled life serve as the example for us as Christians today? Many answer that question in the negative, because to them becoming like Jesus simply give us a list of options from His example from which we can pick and choose depending on our lifestyle, available time for, or willingness? In other words, can I be a true Christian without any signs of progress toward discipleship or spiritual maturity? Is the Lordship of Christ optional or mandatory? While the terms Christian and disciple are synonyms, sadly, many of us separate them. To much of the

American church discipleship is no longer required to be a Christian – similarly, some believe you are not required to be a saint to be a Christian. Many people give that old sheepish grin of distinction, if addressed as either a disciple or a saint. Both issues would probably fall under the category: "Silent issues of the church." Yet, this is a very troubling situation facing the church. Before we go on let us review a couple of observations from the Old Testament in chapter one of this book:

- Abel's sacrifice also contained the shedding of blood, which is – what God requires (Genesis 4:4).
- Cain's sacrifice was bloodless, which is – what humanity is willing to offer God (Genesis 4:3).

Again, where did the example for the blood sacrifice come from? It came from God Himself. Since Cain was the oldest, I am sure Adam taught them both about how God killed innocent animals to make tunics to cover their nakedness. Cain gave God what he was willing to offer – not what God requires (see Genesis 4). Sadly, in traditional and institutional churches today, many pastors are like Cain's religion thousands of years ago, offering God what they are willing to give Him, not what He requires.

- I stated earlier, much of the American church has concluded that one is not required to be, or intended to be, a disciple in order to be a Christian – and one may remain a Christian without any signs of spiritual progress toward discipleship – just be good.
- I repeat many believers are leaving the institutional [religion] church because of a lack of spiritual growth – they want to be fed nourishing spiritual food [truth of the Word] that they may grow thereby. They are leaving to preserve what they do have.
- As earlier stated, there is a grave difference between institutional religion and the faith once delivered to the saints (Jude 3).

It is later than we think. It is definitely not the time for business as usual. I pray that the devastation of COVID-19, and the unstable racial atmosphere lead us to a new spiritual awakening in America. Now is the time for us to rise up and be the church. We should see what God is doing in restoring the apostolic and join Him! The very future of Christianity demands it!

SECTION II

OBEDIENCE IS BETTER THAN SACRIFICE

(OBEDIENCE)

CHAPTER FOUR

OBEDIENCE IS BETTER THAN SACRIFICE

For by the grace given me I say to every one of you: Do not think of yourself more highly than you ought, but rather think of yourself with sober judgment, in accordance with the measure of faith God has given you (Romans 12:3).

Paul compared the church to a human body. There are many members, each with a different function, but all are interrelated and needful to fulfill the various ministries or gifts in the church according to the measure of faith given them. When all members are properly operating in their assigned spiritual gifts the health and unity of the church through the power of the Holy Spirit will glorify God (I Cor. 12:12-31).

We are to be ever mindful that it is only in Jesus Christ that any true spiritual unity in the church can be realized. In verse 3, Paul is clearly begging for humility. Humble is the way. Additionally, he stresses that there will be no grounds for pride, no I am better than you attitude, nor pharisaical self-righteousness. I emphasized pride along with humility because they are opposites. The Bible says, "pride goes before the fall."

In I Samuel 15, we find the rejection of King Saul as king over God's people; in this O.T. narrative within 35 verses we see Saul set before the people as God's king. Before we get to verse 35, God has rejected Saul as king. What went wrong?

- Israel, a theocracy under Jehovah God demanded a king like the other nations (I Samuel 8:4).
- God gives them Saul (see chapter 10-14).
- King Saul established his sovereignty over Israel (14:47).
- Saul is rejected as king (chapter 15).

Jehovah God had been King of Israel and had cared for the nation since its beginning, but the elders of the nation wanted a king to lead them. Among their motivations was that Israel wanted to be like the other nations and have a king to honor. Here we have an example of God's permissive will. He granted their request, but He warned them of the *cost*. Moses anticipated the time when the people would ask for a king and here gave an explicit prophesy of the event:

"When you come to the land which the Lord your God is giving you, and possess it and dwell in it, and say, *'I will set a king over me like all the nations that are around me, 'you shall surely set a king over you whom the Lord your God chooses, one from among your brethren you shall set as king over you; you may not set a foreigner over you, who is not your brother. But he shall not multiply horses for himself, nor cause the people to return to Egypt to multiply horses, for the LORD has said to you, 'You shall not return that way again.' Neither shall he multiply wives for himself, lest his heart turn away, nor shall he greatly multiply silver and gold for himself.*

"Also, it shall be, when he sits on the throne of his kingdom, that he shall write for himself a copy of this law in a book, from the one before the priests, the Levites. And it shall be with him, and he shall read it all the days of his life, that he may learn to fear the LORD his God and be careful to observe all the words of this law and these statutes, that his heart may not be lifted above his brethren, that he may not turn aside from the commandment to the right hand or to the left, and that he may prolong his days in his kingdom, and his children in the midst of Israel" (Deuteronomy 17:14-20).

Even though Samuel objected, they still wanted a king! Even though God *called them* to be separate – from the other nations. Chapter 9 explains how Saul was brought to Samuel and privately anointed king. Note Saul's *humility* in 9:21, and also in 10:22 wherein he hesitated to stand before the people. In 10:8, Samuel instructed Saul to "tarry at Gilgal" wait for Me [when Saul would have his army] – this happened a couple of years later (read chapter 13).

The beginning of the end

Now the time had arrived [10:8] that King Saul was to meet Samuel at Gilgal, He had now established his sovereignty over Israel. Saul had everything going for him, He had:

1) a strong body, 10:23
2) a humble mind, 9:21
3) a new heart 10:9
4) spiritual power 10:10,
5) loyal friends, 10:26; and
6) the guidance and prayers of Samuel

In spite of these advantages, he failed because he would not allow God to be Lord of his life. After a series of sinful failures due to pride, idolatry, and disobedient actions that revealed the darkness of his heart. God removed him! What happened to Saul?

- Saul thought more highly of himself than he should have. He showed great **[pride]** after establishing his sovereignty over Israel. In spite of all the things he had going for him above – he had a monument **[idolatry]** built in his honor (15:12).
- He grew **[impatient]** waiting [seven days] on Samuel to come and offer sacrifices. So, he decided to offer the burnt offering himself **[disobedience]** (study carefully chapters 12-15).
- God was gracious and gave Saul an opportunity to redeem himself through *obedience*. God commanded King Saul to bring complete and total annihilation of the Amalekites (everything that breathed). The Amalekites became a marked people when they attacked Israel in the desert as they left Egypt. God's judgment was severe on those who would destroy His people.

His judgment was <u>equally severe</u> for those who <u>disobeyed His Word</u>. For example, see Achan in Joshua 15:24. God commanded Saul, *"Now go and attack, and* **utterly destroy** *all that they have, and* **do not spare them**. *But kill both man and woman, infant and nursing child, ox and sheep, camel and donkey"*(15:3).

- Note what Saul did with the command given him by God, *"And Saul took Agag, king of the Amalekites* **alive,** *and utterly destroyed all the people with the edge of the sword.* **But Saul** *and the people* **spared Agag and the best of the sheep, the oxen, the fatlings, the lambs,** <u>**and**</u> **with everything despised and worthless – they utterly destroyed** (15:8,9).

- Notice in (v. 20) Saul's response when confronted by Samuel. *"I have obeyed the voice of the Lord......"* He either ignorantly or out of pure deceit maintained that he did what was commanded. Rather than, confessing his sin and repenting, Saul continued to justify himself. He tried to justify his sin by blaming the people and further trying to excuse himself by saying the animals would be used to *sacrifice* to the Lord.

- Samuel's response to Saul was, *"to obey is better than sacrifice."* This is an *essential* Old Testament truth. The OT sacrificial system was never intended *to be a substitute* for living an obedient life marked by heart obedience (study carefully Micah 6:6-8; Hosea 6:6; Amos 5:21-27).

There is no wiggle room

Taking Agag hostage rather than killing him was a direct violation of the Lord's command (v. 3). By sparing Agag and the best of the spoil, Saul was following his own *selfish* desires instead of *serving* as an agent of God's judgment. Perhaps he wanted to gain prestige by bringing home Agag, the king of the Amalekites and the best animals as spoils. Add to that his victories of war with the Philistines.

In fact, Saul went on to Carmel and erected a monument (for himself). Like so many of us today, he needed to see that his *real worship* was indicated by his behavior which reflected his *true* character. He showed himself to be an idolater <u>whose idol was himself.</u> Saul had failed the [humility test] conditions (2:13-15) which would have brought blessings on the nation. His disobedience here was on the same level as witchcraft and idolatry – sins worthy of death! ***A universal principle*** is given here that – those who continually **reject God** will one day **be rejected** by Him. Saul's sins caused God to immediately dispose him and his descendants forever from the throne of Israel.

God is a righteous Judge

To be sure, the Scriptures are clear that God is a righteous judge, and there are times when He pours out His wrath on the earth. And sometimes He judges us by giving us over to our sins. "And even as they did not like to retain God in their knowledge, God gave them over to a debased mind, to do these things which are not fitting; being filled with all unrighteousness, sexual immorality, wickedness, covetousness, maliciousness, full of envy, murder, strife, deceit, evil-mindedness; they are whisperers, backbiters, haters of God, violent, proud, boasters, inventors of evil things, disobedient to parents, undiscerning, untrustworthy, unloving, unforgiving, unmerciful; who knowing the righteous judgment of God, that those who practice such things are deserving of death, not only do the same thing but also approve of them who practice them" (Romans 1:28-32).

Based on this New Testament text it is evidence of God's judgment in our society. Bells should be ringing in our heads when we read such Scriptures as this. Paul did not point a finger at the flagrant sinners, but at the whole human race, which includes us, outside of grace. We are all guilty and worthy of judgment (see Romans 3:23).

Repent or perish

Jesus addressed this, "There were present at that time some who told Him of the Galileans whose blood Pilate had mingled with their sacrifices. Jesus answered, "Do you suppose that these Galileans were worse sinners than all the other Galileans, because they suffered such things? I tell you, no! But unless you *repent*, you will likewise perish. Or those eighteen, upon whom the tower in Siloam fell and killed them, do you think that they were worse offenders than all men living in Jerusalem? I tell you no! But unless you *repent*, you will all likewise perish" (Luke 13:1-5).

Jesus' point is, it is easy to look at someone who died in an unusual or gruesome death and believe such. I remember such an incident as a boy, a lady who was killed in her home by an invader with a butcher knife, it was the talk of the town especially how her blood was spattered all over the room. She had a boyfriend, and both were members of a local church. I remember hearing some of the grownups claiming, "She got what she deserved." Jesus says, "Not so!"

All of us, outside of His mercy, are worthy of judgment, both in this world and in the world to come. Of course, we see in the Old and the New Testaments how God brings judgment on sinning individuals for example: Nadab and Abihu in the Old Testament (see Leviticus 10:1-3) and Ananias and Sapphira in the New Testament (see Acts 5:1-11). This is probably one of the reasons Paul stressed that all Christians should seek and desire the gift of discernment.

While there are differing views surfacing among some Church leaders as to what caused the coronavirus – I am sure we all agree that God is using it to serve as a "wake up call" for His Church! It can also be a signal for change. Additionally, it shines a light on the true gospel message [Christ crucified, buried, and His resurrection] and the need for the churches to repent and return to preaching and teaching the true gospel accompanied by proper behavior and action. Every Christian must witness evangelize as opportunities are presented. It is important that we find out what God is doing, then align ourselves with Him!

CHAPTER FIVE

WHY DISOBEY THE WORD OF THE LORD?

"When you were little in your own eyes, were you not head of the tribes of Israel? And did not the Lord anoint you king over Israel? Now the Lord sent you on a mission, and said, "Go, and utterly destroy the sinners, the Amalekites, and fight against them until they are consumed. Why then did you not obey the voice of the Lord?" (I Samuel 15:17-19).

The question Samuel asked of Saul above can be asked of many pastors and churches today. People continue to pick and choose what part of the faith [*whole body of truth*] once delivered to the saints they are willing to obey. Christ commissioned the whole body of Christ to engage in this mission [the Great Commission] until He returns. He did not suggest this work of the church, He commanded it, based upon His absolute, sovereign authority – Lord of all (see Philippians 2:9-11).

The Great Commission

"Go therefore and make disciples of all nations, baptizing them in the name of the Father and of the Son and of the Holy Spirit, teaching them to observe all things that I have commanded you; and lo, I am with you always, even to the end of the age" (Matthew 28:19-20).

"Go into all the world and preach the gospel to every creature. He who believes and is baptized will be saved, but he who does not believe will not be condemned" (Mark 16:15-16).

"But you shall receive power when the Holy Spirit has come upon you; and shall be witnesses to Me in Jerusalem, and in all Judea and Samaria, and to the end of the earth" (Acts 1:8).

Only disciples can make other disciples

"Making disciples" is a command from our Sovereign Lord and Savior, Jesus Christ that many local churches have determined to be antiquated, obsolete, and no longer needed in choosing their institutional religion over biblical truth. The proper model for making disciples today is the same as the early apostolic church. The process is highly relational that older mature Christians model before their families and community as they mentor a new generation of believers. An older generation becomes models of godliness that invest their lives into a new generation. The older, more mature believers give of their experience to the younger believers, and the younger believers seek after the wisdom of their mentors. Together the church equips people to become *disciples* who make disciples. Though not seen as often as it should be, but there are transformed believers in Christ who:

- Embody what the redeemed church of believers looks like.
- Are authentic models of love.
- Are meeting the needs of hurting people around them.
- Are reconciling the lost to God.
- Are equipping the saints to reproduce themselves spiritually.

When you see the above characteristics working in a local body, you are seeing Jesus' church alive and well in the world. Quite natural these believers may not be expressing all of these elements perfectly, but you are seeing an expression of Christ living through His people. Like Abel they give God what He requires (see Genesis 4; Romans 5:9,10).

First of all, making disciples is not the same as making members, which to many churches simply mean to add names to the church roll. Many people have chosen to withdraw from such churches to maintain their own spirituality. Others feel such churches have left their first love (see Revelation 2:1-4). Like Cain such churches give to God what they want Him to have (see Genesis 4; Revelation 3:14-18):

- They have chosen institutional bloodless religion which means supporting an institution that is part civil religion and part club where religious people share the same politics, dress, worldview, and lifestyles.
- They deny the Holy Spirit and His gifts and ministries.
- They lack spiritual and mature people in leadership.
- Many truly born-again men and women of the faith are leaving the institutional church to preserve their Christian life.
- Young people are leaving the churches and not returning later as did past generations – because the church is not reality to them today.
- The lack of discipleship.
- The lack of spiritual disciplines that support holy and sanctified living.
- Their visions are not aligned with the biblical narrative.
- They have little orthodoxy theology.
- Strategies do not support NT purpose.
- Their Institutional Church doctrines and methodologies [religion] are not biblically supported.
- Their rejection of obedience to the Lord's commands is really rejection of God, Jesus Christ, the Holy Spirit and the people of God.

Since the turn of the century, we have been witnessing the emergence of a new world. The church of Jesus Christ has for the past two decades moved well into the postmodern world. Its worldly influenced expression is more different than most people realize or may care to imagine. I think the scale of the shift is ranking up there with the transitions of the ancient church to the medieval church, then from the medieval church to the modern church and today from the modern church to the postmodern church.

The emerging society has been tagged as post-Christian, pre-Christian, or postmodern. The natural world is profoundly different than it was at the middle of the twentieth century and due to the present coronavirus crisis, even the church culture is changing – just how far the church has retreated can be determined by the lack of voice [conversation] and participation in the present-day crisis. It is well-noted in every briefing that all official decisions are to be made based solely on science and facts. I cannot recollect God even getting a favorable mention in the media, government, or the secular public square in the past twelve months. Every conclusion was reached, and action executed from worldly wisdom, natural power and human strength. We hear the "post Christian cry" in every quarter, "We will get through this together!" Thank goodness is permissible even in the media – But thank God or thank you Jesus! [taboos]

The High Price of Sin

In every quarter of this country, people are waking up to the fact that this nation has lost its way. In each election we elect many religious people to congress. Not long afterward, the people are dissatisfied, because those elected cannot do anything to slow down the sexual immorality, political, societal, and cultural corruption, which if not countered will lead to the death of this nation. The History books are filled with past mighty men and women, mighty nations and mighty civilizations that met their demise because of moral corruption. We just do not seem to get it! The answers we seek are not found in political parties, government institutions, fraternal organizations, nor social reform. God *created* government to obey the laws of God. When He is left out of decisions made on behalf of the people – sin abounds. The price of sin is high!

Believers must face all of life's challenges with trust in God and faithful adherence to His standards as set down in His Word [the Bible]. God *created* the nation of Israel to be His own treasure through which He could show His love, blessings, protection, and example of what it means to be the people of God to the people and nations around them. Israel rejected Him and His plan, as they began to serve idols that they could see and a king to lift up like the other nations (see 2 Kings 17:7). Sin always corrupts and if left unchecked the results are always the same: pain and suffering, heartache, ruin, destruction and death (see Romans 6:23).

The Scripture says, "Do not be deceived, God is not mocked; for whatever a man sows, that he will also reap. For he who sows to his flesh will of the flesh reap corruption, but he who sows to the Spirit will of the Spirit reap everlasting life" (Galatians 6:7-8).

DEATH IS ULTIMATELY THE WAGES OF SIN!

The truth of the matter is we need only to look in the mirror to see the effects of original sin. My family, your family, and each of us personally suffer the fallout of our own sin. The apostle Paul sums it up for us, *"that all people whether Jews or Gentiles, are under the power of sin"* (Romans 3:9).

He then went on to quote this passage from the Old Testament, saying, *"No one is good – not even one. No one has real understanding; no one is seeking God. All have turned away from God; all have gone wrong. No one does good, not even one"* (Romans 3:19-12).

There is a way out of the mundane

As we fully return to our local churches, I pray that we are not looking forward to *"going back to the [same old mundane],"* giving God what you want Him to have. But to give what God requires, a Christ and Bible Centered Church that prioritizes: *"The Great Commandment"* and *"The Great Commission" "preparing our people for the rapture"* and winning others to Christ. Impossible? No! Paul tells us the apostolic way out in Galatians 5:16 to, "Walk in the Spirit."

God is raising up an army of people worldwide who
know that no weapon formed against us shall prosper.
'When the enemy comes in like a flood, the Spirit of the
Lord will raise up a standard against him" (Isaiah 59:19).

No matter how bad it looks – one word can turn a situation around. All it takes is one word from God to change the whole situation. All *true* believers have the presence of the indwelling Holy Spirit as the personal power for pleasing God. Walk indicates a continuous or habitual lifestyle as the believer submits to the Spirit's control. That is, he or she responds in *obedience* to the simple commands of Scripture – growing in their spiritual life (study carefully: Romans 8:13; Ephesians 5:18; Colossians 3:16).

Is COVID-19 the judgment of God?

Over the past 10 months, a number of explanations have been offered concerning the cause of the coronavirus. Some suggest it is a pestilence like those in the Old Testament for our sin. Others say, it is divine judgment from God for our gross national immorality and then there are those who say it is God's judgment on this nation for 60 million aborted babies. When disaster strikes, we all have an initial reaction to it. It may be shock, confusion, or sorrow. Some may secretly think the disaster is a result of sin in the lives of the victims. Let us take a moment to see how Jesus handled a similar question below?

Repent or perish

The coronavirus epidemic is not unique as a wake-up call for all of us to *repent* and *realign* our lives with the infinite plan of God. In fact, all-natural disasters whether hurricanes, floods, fires, famines, locust or diseases – are God's summons to *repent* individually and corporately. This is quite evident as mentioned in an earlier section, the way Jesus responds to the people's inquiries concerning the disaster in (Luke 13:1-5):

> *There were present at that season some who told Him about the Galileans whose blood Pilate had mingled with their sacrifices. And Jesus answered and said to them, "Do you suppose that these Galileans were worse sinners than all other Galileans because they suffered such things? I tell you, no: but unless you repent you will all likewise perish. Or those eighteen on whom the tower fell and killed them; do you think that they were worse sinners than all other men who dwelt in Jerusalem? I tell you no; but unless you repent you will all likewise perish."*

Two disastrous events: Pilate had slaughtered worshippers in the temple and the tower in Siloam had collapsed and killed eighteen people. The crowds wanted Jesus to explain the meaning of these two disasters. In His explanation Jesus relates both events to everyone, not just the ones who died. He says, "No, those killed by Pilate and those who were killed by the falling tower were no worse sinners than – you are." Me? Why does Jesus bring up *their* sin? We didn't ask Him about our sin. They were concerned about the others, the victims not us! That is what makes Jesus' answer stand out. What Jesus said was, the meaning of these two disasters – is for *everyone*. The message is "Repent or perish." He expressed it twice:

- "Except you repent, you will likewise perish" (Luke 13:3).
- "Except you repent, you will likewise perish" (Luke 13:5).

The crowd was astonished that people were so cruelly murdered and crushed so meaninglessly. However, Jesus says, "What you ought to be amazed about is that *you* were not the ones murdered and crushed. In fact, if you do not repent – you yourselves will stand a judgment just like that someday." What we all must think about is that we are all sinners on our way to judgment like that someday.

The word repent in the New Testament means a change
of heart and mind. Not the superficial change of
opinion, accepted by many – but a deep transformation.

Jesus is saying, don't worry about the dead – this is about you, the living and your sins as well. Disasters such as the coronavirus is a message of mercy from God to the whole world to repent and be saved while there is yet time. God has extended much more grace and mercy toward this country than others. Yet, like old Israel, America is ignoring all of the warning signs. God has supplied the answer in His Word:

"If My people who are called by My name will humble themselves, and pray and seek My face, and turn from their wicked ways, then I will hear from heaven, and will forgive their sin and heal their land" (II Chronicles 7:14).

CHAPTER SIX

A CALL TO HUMILITY IN SERVICE

"For whoever exalts himself will be humbled, and he who humbles himself will be exalted" (Luke 14:11; 18:14).

"Humble yourself in the sight of the Lord, and He shall lift you up" (James 4:10).

"Therefore, humble yourselves under the mighty hand of God, that He may exalt you in due time" (1 Peter 5:6).

According to Micah 6:8, humility is necessary to the *service* of the Lord – additionally, our *total dependence* on God is the basis for all genuine blessings. Jesus humbled Himself unto death and opened the *one* and *only* way in which we are to walk. Just as there was no way for Jesus to prove His surrender to God and rise up out of His *human nature* to the glory of God – but through *death;* so, it is with us. Humility must lead us to die to self. This position pronounces a death sentence on *everything relating to self or ego*. Paul set the standard when he said, "Not I, but Christ" (Galatians 2:20). It is either Christ or nothing! This frees us from our fallen nature and leads to life in God – and the full *new nature* of which humility is the very breath. Those churches dedicated to humility in their ministry will not be the most popular stop on Sunday morning.

Where God is all – self is nothing!

Andrew Murray

This is not the crowd's choice, because they are seeking something that satisfies the flesh. Something funny to make them laugh, entertain them, to massage them and make them feel good about themselves.

Those who do come and stay possess a thirsty and sumptuous appetite for God and desire above all else to see Christ glorified in their lives. The glory of God always comes at the sacrifice of self. I would rather be in a setting of two or three gathered in His name to honor God with 100% of the glory, than a stadium full of people seeking entertainment.

Today more and more churches are choosing to put less emphasis on the importance of death to self, which creates a church culture that underestimates the *power* of self. Unless countered, self will distract, deceive, and ultimately fall into compromise of biblical Christianity. The old self must go in its entirety! There is nothing redeemable in it. No matter how much the old self is cleansed and cultured, it is still rotten and unredeemable to its core.

To some churches and some people foreign and domestic, humility is normally identified with penance and remorse for sin. In Central and South American countries during Holy week and Easter a common sight is to see men mutilating their bodies with sharp blades, some are even crucified, and others are beat with thirty-nine strips – all are religious rituals humbly offered as penance for their sins. Though we may not mutilate our bodies with sharp blades, there are works and things established in the institutional religion many churches practice in the name of humility and penance. However, that humility is foreign to biblical humility.

BIBLICAL HUMILITY IS THE REPLACEMENT OF **SELF** BY **CHRIST** ON THE THRONE OF OUR HEARTS!

In Jesus' teaching and in the Epistles, humility is often taught without the mention of sin. Humility is the replacement of *self* by the enthronement of Christ in our hearts. The new believer is in Christ; therefore, has the new divine nature in him or her. So, from this point on we reckon ourselves to be dead to sin – but alive to Christ. The apostle Paul counsels, "What shall we say then?

- Shall we continue in sin that grace may abound? Certainly not! How shall we who died to sin live any longer in it? Or do you not know that as many of us as were baptized into Christ Jesus were baptized into His death?
- Therefore, we were buried with Him through baptism into death, that just as Christ was raised from the dead by the glory of the Father, even so we also should walk in *newness* of life" (Romans 6:1-4).
- Since we are *now* united by faith with Christ, as water baptism symbolizes, His death and burial become ours. If we have died and were buried with Him, we have also been united with Him in His resurrection! Praise God!

There is a new quality and character to our lives – a new *principle* of life! Sadly, this **principle** is not prioritized detailed teaching in local churches. In regeneration the believer is given a new *divine nature* whereby sin describes the old life and righteousness describes the new life (see Ezekiel 36:26; 2 Corinthians 5:17; Galatians 6:15; Ephesians 4:24). A change has come!

Remember! Methods change but principles remain the same!

We will do it our way

This is an important point of consideration with the many churches closed during the coronavirus pandemic. Many cannot wait to get back to their old routine of entertainment and institutional religion. This is a great time to examine ourselves to insure we are in the faith. What changes do we need to execute to be relevant or pertinent to the needs of the people? Are we really a New Testament church? Are we obeying the Lord concerning the Great Commandment and Great Commission – or is this just some more of our voluntary disobedience?

Many churches refuse to change because "we have always done it like that!" In many cases, we continue the tradition knowing that what we are doing is wrong! Others chide, "It works for us!" I hear some pastors complain, "no matter how hard I preach the people are leaving the church through dropout, or transfer – but no additions. As a church, are we asking ourselves why? When you ask about what they are doing about discipleship and witness evangelism, the churches' real purpose – many will retreat in frustration. Why? Knowing that because many of the means [i.e., programs and fund-raisers] in their churches have become the ends by tradition – they cannot be changed. Therefore, tradition uproots and negates sound biblical principles and teaching.

Instead of preaching sermons that challenge or *"stir up your pure minds by way of remembrance"* (2 Peter 3:1), more and more preachers entertain the congregation with the latest forms of entertainment available to capture the attention of poor, immature, underdeveloped Christians. If a local church decides to put away the entertainment and focus on Spirit-led Biblical preaching and teaching; the crowd would immediately flee to another church, one that makes them laugh and helps improve the all-important self-esteem issues they may have. A church that helps us to feel good or better about ourselves – is for many people the goal of religion. This "feel good or better Christianity" is institutional religion. This religion has created a new industry of religious self-help for the well-being of the "self." Their form of Christianity is not rooted in biblical truth, but in cultural relativity – but woe be to the church that is not relevant to the surrounding culture.

Humility, the believer's way to service

In the last section we saw that true humility happens when self is dethroned and Christ rules on the throne of our hearts. The Psalmist said, "I was born in sin and shaped in iniquity." So, "I" was shaped at birth. "I" was born selfish and when hungry "I" cried until "I" was fed. I or me, or myself, or my old adamic self-demanded attention and mom had to give-up and come and feed me to make me smile and feel good. So, from the cradle to the grave, and in all of life – it is natural and expected for "self" to rule or be in charge [me].

As Christians, we have wasted precious time battling "self." No matter our good intentions – self-rules! We underestimate the power of "self" to compromise true biblical Christianity through distraction and deception – in order to control our lives. In Galatians 2:20, the apostle Paul set the standard – Not I but Christ! The old self must go! Remember, we cannot educate it, polish it up, so, all we can do is bring an end to it.

The old man was crucified with Christ. The new man is now in Christ as stated earlier so, from now on you must reckon your**self** to be **dead to sin** but alive to God in Jesus Christ. Knowing this, according to the Word of God – now that self is gone; I am now fit for Christ's service! This teaching needs to be prioritized, if you want to enter full fellowship with Christ in His death, and know fully the deliverance from self, *humble* yourself. This is the command to all of us! A believer is not the same person he or she was prior to conversion and is therefore a *new* creation (2 Corinthians 5:17).

We do all to the glory of God in service, and we know that God will not share His glory! He commands all the glory! Self would be pleased to hang on to even a minute "bit." But God is not pleased even with that "bit" of disobedience, a lack of true humility. How do I deal with the old self?

First of all, the death to self is God's work. Remember, the life in you has gone through the process of *death* and *resurrection*. If we claim and receive the fulness of Christ, which can maintain His death to self and sin in its full power – makes humility the overcoming spirit of our lives.

Putting the old man [self] to death

Adam and Eve rejected God's original design for our character in the Garden of Eden. As Adam's descendants, we bore his image, an image of God which had become distorted because of Adam's sin. But as we walk in God's light, we are transformed into the image of His Son Jesus Christ, *"the last Adam."* We walk by faith so; in faith we claim the death and life of Jesus as your own. Let a loving humility mark you as one who has claimed your birthright – the baptism into the death of Christ.

"By one offering He hath perfected forever them that are sanctified" (Hebrews 10:14).

Those entering Christ's humiliation will find *in Him* the power to see and reckon themselves dead to self – and have learned and received of Him to walk with all lowliness bearing one another's burdens in love and life with humility like that of Christ.

---

*"Yield yourselves unto God as alive from
the dead"* (Romans 6:3, 11, 13).

What was lost through Adam's sin, Jesus desires to *restore* through you and me by His Spirit.

SECTION III

THE APOSTOLIC RISING

(SERVICE)

CHAPTER SEVEN

TOTAL FULFILLMENT IN CHRIST ALONE

"In the beginning was the Word and the Word was with God, and the Word was God. He was in the beginning with God. All things were made through Him, and without Him nothing was made that was made. In Him was life, and the life was the light of men" (John 1:1-4). *"And I will pray the Father, and He will give you another Helper, that He may abide forever – the Spirit of truth ….. He dwells with you and will be in you"* (John 14:16-17).

The search for something real is not new. It has been going on since the very beginning of history. People have looked for reality and satisfaction in wealth, conquest, power, learning – and even religion. There is nothing really wrong with them, except alone or by themselves they never reach fulfilment. John had discovered and shares a truth that still rings true today after two-thousand years, that satisfying fulfilment or reality is not found in materialism or hedonism, but only in a Person – Jesus Christ.

Christ, this Life revealed

In his writings John makes it clear that we do not have to search for this life in Christ, because it was manifested or revealed openly! God revealed Himself in creation (see Romans 1:20), but for His love to be fully revealed required more. God also has revealed Himself much more fully in His Word – the Bible. But praise God, His final and most complete revelation is in His Son, Jesus Christ. Jesus said, "He that hath seen Me hath seen the Father" (John 14:9). KJV As God's revelation of Himself, Jesus has an incredibly special name: "The Word of Life" (1 John 1:1). Jesus, The Word of Life, promised us abundant life. Why are we so willing to settle for less? Over time we have stopped aiming at the hearts of people with our spiritual "education" in order to hit their heads. We have believed that if we feed people enough Bible information it will automatically transform their lives. Wrong!

The devil knows more Bible than most local church
members in this country, and can authenticate
our doctrinal statements, but after 2000 years
this knowledge has not transformed him.

Jesus told the Pharisees that they did not get the point in their study of the Scriptures.

---

*"You search the Scriptures, for in them you think you have
eternal life; and these are they which testify of Me. But you are not
willing to come to Me that you may have life"* (John 5:39-40).

Jesus was pointing out that with their studious efforts, they had miserably failed in their understanding of the true way to eternal life through the Son of God. They searched for eternal life, but were not willing to trust its only source, Jesus Christ. The point He is making here is those people who receive eternal life are identified as those who hear the Word and believe in the Father and the son. They are the people who have eternal life and never will be condemned. *"There is therefore now no condemnation to those who are in Christ Jesus who do not walk according to the flesh, but according to the Spirit"* (Romans 8:1).

The Holy Spirit, and the Life revealed

The apostle John speaks of the Holy Spirit as the Comforter, and Helper, "one *literally* called alongside" (John 14:16) namely one of the same as Jesus, who extends the ministry of Jesus until the end of this age. Therefore, the Holy Spirit fulfills a definite function or role in relation to Jesus Christ. While the Father sent the Holy Spirit in the name of Christ, the Spirit never draws attention to Himself, nor does He speak in His own authority. Instead, His *mission* is to glorify Jesus Christ and to declare His teachings to the disciples (16:14).

Today the Holy Spirit and His work has been replaced in many local churches with a counterfeit religion and entertainment(ism) that denies the supernatural and simply implements entertaining self-help programs instead of true apostolic spiritual worship and ministry. Some Christians consider the Holy Spirit a mere influence, feeling, impersonal force, or other misconception that causes much ignorance and confusion in the body of Christ. Such disruptions counter a true relationship with Him. Without the Holy Spirit and His gifts and ministries there can be no true Apostolic New Testament Church. Peter gave the message when asked the question, "What shall we do:" He said to them, "Repent, and let every one of you be baptized in the name of Jesus Christ for the remission of sins; and you shall receive the gift of the Holy Spirit. For the promise is to you and to your children, and to all who are afar off, as many as the Lord our God will call" (Acts 2:38-39).

"But you shall receive power when the Holy Spirit has come upon you; and you; shall be witnesses to Me in Jerusalem, and in Judea, and Samaria, and to the end of the earth" (Acts 1:8).

Therefore, it is imperative that individual Christians and the local churches realize this commission from Christ absolutely necessitates the Holy Spirit in the entire life of the believer and the entire operation of the church.

The necessity of the Holy Spirit in individual Christians

- The Holy Spirit in tandem with the Word of God brings about the "new birth" (see John 3:3, 5-6).
- The Holy Spirit *indwells* the true born-again New Testament saints; undoubtedly that is the major difference between them and Old Testament saints, wherein the Holy Spirit *came upon* them for certain services (see Romans 8:9; 1 Corinthians 3:16; 6:17; I John 2:27).
- The Holy Spirit guides the believer into all truth and all of life (John 16:13)
- The Holy Spirit convicts the individual (John 16:8).
- The Holy Spirit directs believers in the service of the Lord (I Corinthians Acts 8:29; 10:19; 16:6-7).
- The Holy Spirit imparts spiritual gifts to the members of the Church severely as He wills (I Corinthians 12:7-11).
- The Holy Spirit empowers the Christian for ministry and witness evangelism (Acts 1:8).
- The Holy Spirit glorifies the Lord Jesus Christ (John 16:14).
- The Holy Spirit will bring about the resurrection and immortality to the true Christians' bodies in the last day (Romans 8:11; I Corinthians 15:47-51; I Thessalonians 4:15-18).

The necessity of the Holy Spirit in the Church

Jesus promised His disciples that the Holy Spirit would come and dwell in them and as the Comforter abide with them forever (John 14:16-17).

Some of the major responsibilities of the Holy Spirit in the Church are:

- The Holy Spirit formed the church into a corporate living organism, the body of Christ on the Day of Pentecost.
- The Holy Spirit baptizes the true believers into the body of Christ (I Corinthians 12:13).
- The Holy Spirit formed the church to be the new and living temple of God, setting believers into their places as living stones in the New Covenant Temple (I Corinthians 3:16; 6:16; Ephesians 2:20-22).

- The Holy Spirit brings the anointing, illumination and direction to the church as the New Covenant Priestly Body of Christ (see II Corinthians 1:21; Psalm 133:1-22; John 2:20, 27; Ephesians 1:17-18; Acts 10:38; 1 Corinthians 12:12-13).
- The Holy Spirits brings spiritual fruit, and spiritual gifts to the members of the church (I Corinthians 12:4-11, 28-31; Romans 12:6-8; Galatians 5:22-23).

The Lord Jesus is the Head of the Church in heaven and directs His affairs in His Body, the Church, through the Holy Spirit. The Spirit is:

- Transforming true believers into the image of Christ.
- Calling, quickening, energizing, and equipping the various ministries in the Church. Calling, quickening, energizing, equipping and placing each member of the Body of Christ as He sees fit (see Acts 13:-13; 15:28; 20:28; 1 Corinthians 12:8-11; Ephesians 4:8-12; 1 Peter 1:12; 1 Corinthians 2:1-5; Acts 1:8). Reading this chapter, I am sure you recognized the tricks and deceptions of Satan to deceive and confuse God's people concerning the Holy Spirit.

In Christ alone

When you are in Christ, you are not just a member in an organization but a part of a living organism. We are the actual body of Christ on earth; *none of us is the head,* but we all form one community, bound together by the Holy Spirit, the same Spirit that raised Jesus from the dead. The power of God, the reign and rule of God is most strongly expressed when we know we are bound together by Jesus Christ, in Jesus Christ, and under Jesus Christ. Out of this unity in Christ there is a diversity of gifts sovereignly given to the members of the body of Christ by the Holy Spirit. The expectation here is not independence, nor dependence, but interdependence. We are just one small part of God's vast kingdom.

> "Why do we divide and tear to pieces the members of Christ and raise up strife against our own body? And why have we reached such a height of madness as to forget that *we are members one of another?*"
>
> Clement of Rome

New places in the Spirit

Church History has recorded times when Christianity met some extremely critical struggles for survival. One of the most desperate times was the eleven hundred years that Roman Catholicism was the depository for Christianity. During this dark age of the church, many of the truths so dear to salvation, eternal life, and growth in the Christian life *were lost.* The Bible was written in a language that the common man did not know. God raised up an apostolic priest, Martin Luther among the Roman Catholic priesthood whom He used as the catalyst to fire up the worldwide Restoration Movement in 1715. He was awakened to the Biblical truth, "The just shall live by faith." This truth burned a hole right through the Roman Catholic Church papacy's non-biblical hierarchy established to replace the early apostolic Church. Through that Reformation period the following truths were restored:

- Justification by faith
- Forgiveness of sin
- The just shall live by faith
- Christ is our only High Priest
- Priesthood of believers
- Eternal life

I am sure many of you are surprised at the list of lost truths. To think, for eleven hundred years forgiveness of sins and eternal life had to be purchased from the church. Every generation and age need their own pioneer including the church. Humans get stuck in the mundane and just remain the same or sometimes revert backward. Pioneers motivate, push the people forward, keep them from complacency and motivate the

---

[9] Gerald Bray and Thomas C. Oden, *Romans,* Ancient Christian Commentary on Scripture: New Testament VI (Dower Grove: InterVarsity Press, 1998), p. 311.

church to reach goals. This apostolic anointing keeps the church from being *outdated* and makes us *relevant* in the world without compromise.

The apostolic like all pioneers are often misunderstood and misquoted. The benefits of their lives are often seen only after they are gone. The early apostles were pioneers, laying the foundation for the Church and writing the New Testament. They were misunderstood and persecuted. And yet because of their apostolic spirit, they overcame obstacles that would have stopped the average man or woman. Without these people, nothing is established for that generation. The apostolic spirit gives the ability to lay foundations for our generation. Without this apostolic dimension a whole generation can be lost!

Therefore, I say with confidence, after years working an apostolic teaching ministry on four Continents. If you are a part of the Church, this book is for you. It is time for the local church everywhere to take stock of this ministry of the apostolic. To take stock means to look it over, study or examine again. Many have studied apostolic ministry from a historical perspective and concluded that the apostolic age of the Church ended with the deaths of the twelve apostles. To them we are living in a day when there are no apostles. In other words, there is no such thing as an apostolic ministry today.

The Holy Spirit, however, is speaking today to many individually and some churches to take another look at the ministry. By doing so:

- We are seeing things that were previously hidden from our view.
- We will see things that we have never seen.
- We will see things that were previously seen in a whole new life.
- Many will want to readjust their thinking and teaching.

The apostle Paul admonishes, "Consider what I say, and may the Lord give you understanding in all things" (2 Timothy 2:7). You cannot receive understanding unless you consider what is being said. Some people are so closed-minded, they will not even entertain the thought that apostolic ministry is for today. Please consider *all of* what I have said in this book – and upon so doing, I pray that the Lord will give you understanding in all things.

CHAPTER EIGHT

THE RENEWED NEW COVENANT COMMUNITY

"This is my body which is given for you. Do this in remembrance of me" (Luke 22:19).

In the same manner he took the cup, saying, *"This cup is the new covenant in my blood. Do this, as often as you drink it in remembrance of me"* (1 Corinthians 11:25).

"This is the covenant which I will make with the house of Israel after those days, says the LORD: I will put my law within them, and I will write it upon their hearts; and I will be their God, and they shall be my people ... for I will forgive their iniquity, and I will remember their sin no more" (Jeremiah 31:33-34).

Once a person receives salvation, the Holy Spirit enters and encourages the new Christian to *go deeper in the faith* and urges him or her to reproduce themselves in others. The idea that *there is a deeper and better Christian life* than most Christians know or are aware of on the resurrection side of the cross. This is a crucial message at this juncture in church history. As pastors we must change our methods to reach and change a postmodern culture *without* changing the timeless message of the gospel of Jesus Christ.

The idea is not new in fact, it was a major concern back in the Old Testament and the experience of Israel. In Israel's obedience in preparation and miraculously being *led* out of Egypt, and across the Red Sea on dry land. Then, led for forty years through the wilderness burying the older post Egypt generation and across the Jordan River, again on dry land and on into the Promised Land with Joshua and Caleb. All the way [God's way] Israel was led by a cloud during the day and a pillar of fire by night. They drank water from a rock, and they were fed bread from heaven. Miracles, miracles, and more miracles were performed daily. The psalmist noted, "there was not a feeble one among them!"

In spite of God's loving care and safe guiding – soon changes began to take place. These changes were not affected by one generation, but over a period of years and several generations. **God sent the prophet to rebuke and call Israel back to center, to follow Jehovah.** Like Israel, over time much of the Church has moved from the center of God's will to the outer extremes [externalism]. The Holy Spirit was replaced with an external ceremony. Church history has recorded various interventions that God has instituted in the world throughout the past two thousand years to call His Church back to the center, to follow Christ – the New Covenant. Rather than seek the Lord's direction day to day, many have become content with what they did yesterday and the day before. Such churches have gotten use to proceeding through life – looking back [rearview mirror] and repeating [a learned behavior] the events of the past, many of which are placed above the Word of God in importance. They follow manmade forms, ceremonies, and traditions, as the local churches celebrate what they once were.

Many times, the only changes are the dates on their current printed programs and bulletins. In many cases the repetition is repeated for generations [slow death]. Soon we are left with a form but no worship. External institutional religion takes over. The form takes many shapes today with entertainment at its core. God wants true worship! **Christ Himself, has called His Church back to center!**

Cultural blending

Looking at a statistical report on the church dated August 2019, reported 8,000 to 10,000 church closures across America that year. Today August 29, 2020, the first question that came to my mind was, "How many are closed because those in control refused to change?" Prior to the shut-down due to the COVID-19 many churches in this country were already knowingly on life support; and yet they still resisted or refused to allow change. Many such churches probably will not survive the virus. I have read of some of the problems occurring in the local for example:

- Significant cuts in tithes and offerings
- Church rolls are down by 50% or more.
- Pastors are experiencing cuts in salary (or no salary)
- Churches are looking for bi-vocational pastors.
- The churches are seeking volunteers to fill some salaried positions.

Unfortunately, too many dying churches contribute to their own death by not being willing to change their ways and means to the positive influence and guidance of the Holy Spirit and the Word of God which would mean a Christ-centered and Bible-centered rather than a man-centered church. Although known indicators of sure death faced these churches and screamed for attention over the past 40 to 60 years, the leaders resisted change and the results are obvious today.

Seven last words of a dying church

There is a growing number of true Christians leaving the organized traditional institutional churches today, because in their own words, they are leaving to maintain their own spiritual life. Many declaring that remaining in such an environment is detrimental to the spiritual growth of their entire families. In earlier days, some people who joined the church were not saved but they used their church affiliation for social status. However, today cultural Christianity is no longer the norm. Prior to COVID-19 more than 35% of the Sunday morning crowd was no longer there because "going to church" is no longer seen as a requirement for social validation. Also, research had shown that two generations were missing from most congregations at that time. Had someone told a congregation in the 1990s how many people sitting there in the pews would not be there in 2021, they would have thought the person was off their rocker. Of course, COVID – 19 has had an impact also.

There is a growing number of people required to work regularly on Sundays. Therefore, they are forced to miss corporate worship due to work requirements. Despite resistance, many local churches will be forced to explore alternative worship times and means to reach those unable to make it on Sundays due to 7-day a week work schedules. In person-worship is biblically commanded and needful (see Hebrews 10:25).

Due to denominational decline especially in churches where traditionally denominations have had a vast amount of influence in pastor placement – churches today have a much greater say in selecting their leaders than in the past. In many cases the spread and growth of institutional religion and resistance to change in traditional churches have often contributed to their detriment and neglect has encouraged new church-planting.

For such a time as this

The church landscape will continue to change especially now and after the COVID-19 epidemic, the non-essential label, and the ["out of sight-out of mind"] mind-set that the culture has placed on the local church are over. Church leaders must be open to necessary cultural change, that is when the church is actually leading the change. I honestly believe God has placed us here for such a time as this. Regardless of your role in God's kingdom, we need to understand these required changes which will affect the survival and meaningful reopening of many of our local churches:

- As a church we must re-consecrate ourselves as living sacrifices holy and acceptable unto God which is our reasonable service – return to the church's mission, the Great Commission and yield fully to the leading of the Holy Spirit and the Word of God.
- Take out time for a critical review of our principles, disciplines and practices to ensure that we are Christ-centered, Bible-based and we must invoke much prayer for wisdom and direction from God above. It is time for us to rediscover the power of prayer ministry in our churches and *be* a difference.

- Once again advance the gospel of Jesus Christ.
- Return to the center of God's will for His church.
- It is past time to "be filled with the Spirit," as commanded and allow the Holy Spirit with His fruit, gifts, and ministries to take His rightful place within us to comfort, lead and guide us into all truth (Ephesians 5:18; Romans 8:14).
- It is time for us to repent and turn back to Jesus Christ. To do so gives us the power, and authority, and the deeper life of "joy unspeakable and full of glory" (1 Peter 1:8).
- One thing we must remember, leadership is being an example to those coming along behind to follow.

Being led of the Spirit

Unfortunately, many Christians born again, and baptized in the Holy Spirit have never developed an intimate *personal* relationship with the Father. They are content with just belonging to the family of God and serving Him *collectively* with their brothers and sisters in the Lord that may be through church attendance, choir, tithing, and even performing good works. They are content. Outwardly, they may be classified as "good Christians." Are they manifested as the sons of God? Or are they simply good old boys. Romans 8:14 says, *"For as many as are led by the Spirit of God, they are the sons of God."* Therefore, indication that Christians are sons of God is the fact that they are led by the Spirit of God. However, too many do not really know what that means. Having the ability to hear the voice of God and then act on it is part of what it means to be led of the Spirit. Being led of the Spirit then is twofold:

1) It is receiving God's instructions.
2) It is obeying and fulfilling the will of God in the spirit (character) of Jesus.

Therefore, the Apostle Paul in Romans 8:29, states that it is God's desire that the *individual* character of His children be transformed and become identical with the *character* of Jesus: *For whom He did foreknow, He also did predestinate to be conformed to the image of His Son, that he might be the firstborn among many brethren.*

> **The heavenly Father wills that His <u>numerous</u> *adopted* sons and [daughters] be conformed to the only *begotten* Son, Jesus Christ.**

Being conformed to the image of Jesus simply means taking on His form; His likeness, His stature or resemblance – when all of God's children are conformed to the *character* and *likeness* of His begotten Son, Jesus. Only then will it become evident that they are led by the Spirit and are therefore truly the sons of God. Developing the character of Jesus is accomplished by developing the same *fruit* that was so easily identifiable in His life.

Jesus taught that it is by outward manifestation (fruit) that inward nature (*character*) is recognized. *"Wherefore by their fruit ye shall know them ..."* (see Matthew 7:15,16,20).KJV Jesus said this as He taught His disciples about false prophets. The world must be able to recognize the true sons of God, as they observe professed Christians. They recognize the false teachers by their fruit! It is amazing the number of churches that undoubtedly think differently. Jesus did not say, "You will know them by their miracles, nor did He say by their speaking in tongues, nor the number of chapters of the Bible they can quote. He said, "You can recognize my disciples by their *character!* (see Galatians 5:22, 23)

Jesus is our Example

In spite of what is plainly written in the Word of God, concerning the Holy Spirit there is much confusion. Luke recorded, after Jesus was baptized, affirmed, empowered and overcame Satan, He began His public ministry <u>under the power of the Holy Spirit</u>:

> *Then Jesus returned in the power of the Spirit to Galilee, and news of Him went out through all the surrounding regions. And He taught in their synagogues, being glorified by all. So, He came to Nazareth, where He had been brought up. And as His custom was, He went into the synagogue on the Sabbath day, and stood up to read. And He was handed the book of the prophet Isaiah. And when He had opened the book, He found the place where it was written: "The Spirit of the LORD is upon Me, because He has*

anointed Me to preach the gospel to the poor; He has sent Me to heal the brokenhearted, to proclaim liberty to the captives and recovery of sight to the blind, to set at liberty those who are oppressed; and proclaim the acceptable year of the Lord" (Luke 4:14-19).

It is especially important to note Luke makes it clear that Jesus would not use His own power or carry out His own plans. Everything Jesus *said* and *did*, <u>He did in surrender and under the Holy Spirit's power and direction.</u> As our ultimate Example, His way of life and ministry coincides with our ministry today:

- Jesus operated under the Spirit's power, not His own [which He had set aside] (v.14).
- Jesus used spiritual gifts to serve – He clearly had the gifts of teaching, miracles, healing, discernment, and raising the dead to name a few.

The Holy Spirit provided what Jesus needed to carry out the Father's purpose on earth. We have the same Holy Spirit within us and the same spiritual gifts that Jesus used – we *can* do the same! Again, Jesus is our Example, He chose to become one of us and one with us by substituting in our stead on the cross. By this choice, He not only made our eternal life possible; but He also made our life *here and now* possible by demonstrating as a human being Himself – how we are to live as people *empowered* by the Holy Spirit.

Every generation of believers since Christ's ascension and Pentecost have had *to be re-educated* to the *truth* that only a Spirit-filled life pleases God. During the Last Supper, Jesus promised and described the Holy Spirit (study carefully John 13-17).

IF WE HAVE THE SAME INDWELLING HOLY SPIRIT JESUS HAD, AND THE CHURCH (UNIVERSAL) HAS THE SAME SPIRITUAL GIFTS HE USED – TOGETHER WE CAN DO WHAT JESUS DID!

It is time that we realize the local church is a living organism and not an organization. Therefore, it is imperative for us to re-align our local churches with Christ and His example through the faith once delivered to the saints (see Jude 3; 1 Corinthians 11:25). This can happen if we repent and return to the churches' first love, God, and secondly others. Then, as obedient children, do what He commanded us to do in the Great Commission; but only under the power, leading, and anointing of the Holy Spirit (Acts 1:8; 2:38-39).

It seems that during the Reformation the priests laid down their ecclesiastical vestments for academic robes moving from priest to Senior Pastor with a hierarchal [pecking order] of *lay* staff in a support role. That makes a church an organization rather than organism. Actually, a pharisaical form mentioned nowhere in the New Testament for the church. What is so appalling with this model? The fact of the matter is much of what we see practiced today cannot be backed up with the New Testament either. In Exodus 18, we find Moses modeling the very ministry style that is such a hindrance to effective pastoral ministry today. It was not good then and it is not good now. God sent Jethro to speak wisdom to Moses: "What you are doing is not good." In other words, Moses no one is questioning your call, your motives, or your gifting – but you cannot do it all." Jethro coached Moses to appoint leaders to oversee groups of 10, 50, 100, and 1000, and take only the most difficult cases himself. In the very next chapter, God declares that all of Israel, not just the Levites, will become priests. In the New Testament the Apostle Peter says of the children of God,

"But you are a chosen generation, a royal priesthood,
a holy nation, His own special people, that you may
proclaim the praises of Him who called you out of darkness
into His marvelous light: who once were not a people
but are now the people of God, who had not obtained
mercy but now have obtained mercy" (1 Peter 2:9).

It is time for us to stop voicing it, and just let the Holy Spirit "have His way" using the graces God has provided through Him for His glory. God's priority puts more emphasis on what we are as we cultivate the fruit of the Spirit (Galatians 5:22-23), than what we do with the gifts of the Spirit (1 Corinthians 12 – 14).

Again, we will reference Moses, God gave him a rod for his work. Over and over again Moses used the rod for the purposes God gave it to him. But he also sinned with this mighty gift from God which he used in the parting of the Red Sea and later before Pharaoh. Though it was a gift from God, the staff could be used for wrong purposes. Christians are quick to say a gift is not of God if *character* is lacking in the person.

We tend to forget that repeatedly throughout the Bible the people God used also had major *character flaws*. Often real gifts are found in *poor containers*. In 2 Corinthians 4, Paul declares that the gift nor the power is from us but from God.

OFTEN REAL GIFTS ARE FOUND IN POOR CONTAINERS.

This is why growing the fruit of the Spirit (character) is especially so important. God wants to use His gifts *through* us while He continues to work on us. Paul begins by saying: *"Now about the gifts of the Spirit, brothers and sisters, I do not want you to be "ignorant"* (1 Corinthians12:1).

This statement forms the biblical foundation for our common understanding of the gifts, in order that we might use and grow in our gifts. Also, notice this statement is directed to the whole church. God gives His gifts to both men and women; gender has nothing to do with God's work through the gifts of the Spirit. Then we will experience the fruit of the Spirit which will allow us to deal with the gift with a right motive, attitude, and understanding. Again, the gifts of the Spirit are undergirded by the fruit of the Spirit and must give a place of developing (character), which is a deep reservoir of love, joy, peace, patience, kindness, goodness, faithfulness, gentleness, and self-control (see Galatians 5:22-23). Any other results may be suspect. In any case, pastors, if things begin to slide as they did in the Corinthian Church, then like Paul, we should provide them with needed correct teaching! Before we intervene by dismissing or stopping a spiritual experience, we need to understand its source – human, satanic, or godly.

Many of these believers at Corinth were *"led astray."* When we worship anyone or any other so-called god; we are placed in *bondage* and condemned to a walk which leads to death. *Trumpism* among many Evangelical Christians today is a good example. That is why we must cherish being led by the Holy Spirit!

CHAPTER NINE

THE APOSTOLIC RISING

"And He Himself gave some to be apostles, some prophets, evangelists and some pastors and teachers, for the equipping of the saints for the work of ministry, for the edifying of the body of Christ, till we all come to the unity of the faith and the knowledge of the Son of God, to a perfect man, to the measure of the stature of the fullness of Christ" (Ephesians 4:11-12).

Christ, the Apostle from heaven (Hebrews 3:1)

In earlier sections we discussed reasons why so many of our local churches are dying at an alarming rate; and so many have silently closed their doors permanently over the past three decades. I personally believe the most important revelation that the church has overlooked or just flat missed since the Reformation of 1517, was the *restoration* and rising of the apostolic and the priesthood of all believers to the churches in the 1990's.

The twelve apostles of the Lamb (Luke 6:12-13)

Apostle is a term used particularly of the twelve disciples who had physically seen the risen Christ including Matthias, who replaced Judas (see Acts 1:22). We all have probably heard the question, "How many apostles were in the Bible?" The answer that comes back 12, and they were called *"the apostles to Christ"* because He chose them (Galatians 1:1; 1 Peter 1:1) and gave them three basic responsibilities:

1) to lay the foundation of the church (Ephesians 2:20).
2) to receive, declare and write God's Word (Ephesians 3:5; Acts 11:28; 21:10,11).
3) to give confirmation of that Word through signs, wonders, and miracles (2 Corinthians 12:12; Acts 8:6-7; Hebrews 2:3, 4).

Then someone might argue, "Well wasn't Paul an apostle?" The conversation continues, "No, because he did not physically see Christ as did the 12." "Well, he did miraculously encounter Jesus at his conversion on the Damascus Road" (Acts 9:1-9; Galatians 1;15-17). The reply, "Well, that does not count! Later, Paul was uniquely set apart as *"the apostle to the gentiles"* (Galatians 1:15-17).

Paul, the apostle to the Gentiles

Sadly, the argument has gone back and forth for nearly 2000 years. In these postmodern times you might get the answer from some people on the church rolls, "Who cares?" "What difference does it make?" "It has worked for us for over 75 years!" Well, my brothers and my sisters, we had better wake up and smell the roses! While we have been arguing about our church doctrine, programs, customs and traditions, Satan has been busy fanning the flames of the churches with doubt and unbelief.

If what you are doing is wrong – why continue to train other generations to do the same?

Jay R. Leach

As a result, many of the local churches have forgotten God, the work of Christ, and has denied the Spirit and the Word of God! At the same time substituting a non-spiritual natural form [a hierarchy/ and institutional religion] which denies biblical purpose and work of the Holy Spirit along with the truth of God's Word. In many institutional churches this deception has been so widely accepted and practiced, it is received as the true.

A New Order [post ascension]

Actually, this whole discussion makes a great deal of difference, especially when we strive to discover the present-day work and ministry of the apostolic. If Paul is an apostle as one of the twelve, he cannot be an example or a pattern for us today of what an apostle is to be. The 12 had their own work and their own function.

However, in 1 Timothy 1:16, Paul did refer to himself as a pattern for the New Testament believer. Paul was saved so God could display to all, His gracious and merciful patience with the most wretched sinners. In verse 15, Paul expresses, that Christ Jesus came into the world to save sinners. Paul's testimony is repeated seven times in the New Testament (study carefully 1 Timothy 1:12-17; Acts 9:22, 26, Galatians 1,2; Philippians 3:1-14). Paul claimed to be the chief of sinners. Yet, his conversion has been instrumental in the salvation of many.

Thus, Paul becomes the first of a new order of apostolic ministry that Christ instituted upon His ascension back to heaven (Ephesians 4:11). We find that there are at least four categories of apostolic ministries, each with specific qualifications and functions of ministries:

1) Christ, the Chief Apostle from heaven, the ultimate pattern by which all apostolic ministries are measured.
2) The twelve apostles of the Lamb chosen by Jesus specifically to lay the initial foundation of His church during the apostolic age, which lasted to the end of the first 100 years of the church.
3) The post-ascension apostolic ministry to which Paul belonged. Upon His ascension to heaven the Scripture says Christ gave this apostolic ministry to the church to build up and equip the saints to full maturity. This order of the apostolic is to function

throughout the church age (Ephesians 4:13). Others who are mentioned in the New Testament apostolic ministry are:

- Andronicus and Junia (see Romans 16:7)
- James, the brother of the Lord (see Galatians 1:19)
- Barnabas (see Acts 4:36; 13:2; 14:14)
- Titus (see 2 Corinthians 8:23)
- Epaphroditus (see Philippians 2:25)
- Timothy and Silvanus (see 1 Thessalonians 1:1; 2:6)
- Apollos (see 1 Corinthians 4:6, 9)

4) Paul serves as an example to those who perform apostolic ministry today, but you *must* first receive a *call* and *be* placed. Ephesians 4:11-13, answers the "how long" question, in reference to the duration of the apostolic *functions* [apostle, prophet, evangelist, pastor, and teacher] that Christ gave to the churches?

"Till we all come to the unity of the faith and of the knowledge of the Son of God, to a perfect man, to the measure of the stature of the fullness of Christ" (Ephesians 4:13).

I do not believe this passage will be a reality until these apostolic leadership ministries (functions) and purpose for which Christ gave them to the church can be fully realized. Today, without spiritual change through the power of the Holy Spirit – to do the job that Christ assigned is impossible! Therefore, those churches without the Holy Spirit will not get needed insight and wisdom. Where there is only a non-spiritual, traditional hierarchy and practice of institutional religion – there is no room for the spiritual. Such churches need spiritual teaching, instruction, insight, revelation, and understanding of the wisdom of God through which the apostolic ministry functions.

The apostle Paul definitely possessed and demonstrated the gifts of the Spirit in his ministry. In fact, it was Paul who brought much of the amazing revelation of these gifts. Perhaps it was during his three years spent in Arabia after his conversion that he moved so deeply into the mysteries of God (Galatians 1:15-18).

Not only did Paul number the gifts, but he named them as well in 1 Corinthians 12. He then gave us the laws for operating them in chapter 14, but you cannot get to the operation of the gifts in chapter 14 without going through love in chapter 13. How could he have the doctrine of the gifts without having the doctrine of the fruit of the Spirit as well (see Galatians 5:22-23)?

In Acts 16, we see Paul manifesting the gift of ***discerning of spirits*** which he admonishes all Christians to desire:

> *And it came to pass, as we went to prayer, a certain damsel possessed with a spirit of divination met us, which brought her masters much gain by soothsaying: the same followed Paul and us, and cried, saying, "These men are the servants of the Most-high God, which show unto us the way of salvation"* (vv. 16-17). But Paul saw an evil spirit in her. Finally, he turned and said to that spirit, *"I command thee in the name of Jesus Christ to come out of her. And he came out the same hour"*(v. 18). KJV

The healing power of God flowed from Paul. He demonstrated the gifts of ***healing*** in Acts 14: *"And there sat a certain man at Lystra, impotent in his feet, being a cripple from his mother's womb, who never had walked"* (v. 8). With a loud voice, Paul said to the man, *"Stand upright on thy feet"* (v.10). Immediately the man leaped and walked.

In Acts 16:25, we see the gift of **faith** demonstrated through Paul, when Paul and Silas are in prison. They had been beaten with stripes and as blood ran down their backs, they had no way to help themselves. Rather than complain the Bible says that at midnight they sang praises to God! The gift of ***faith*** began to function as the old jail began to shake, their bonds dropped off and the doors flung open; and the jailer fell to his knees, wanting to know what he must do to be saved. That night not only the jailer but his entire family were saved and baptized. They heard the gospel and received it in their hearts. Not only did Paul present and teach us the broad scope of all these beautiful gifts, but as stated earlier, he allowed them to function in his own life. We have just touched on the subject of gifts. I challenge you to seek God for these major gifts. We read in 1 Corinthians 12:31, we are to *"covet earnestly the best gifts."* An in-depth study of Paul's writings would reveal a wealth of information as to how the gifts functioned in his life and apostolic ministry.

A major task of the apostolic miniseries today is to *re-establish true foundational* apostolic functions in the body of Christ. This is what the apostle Paul was establishing and correcting in the first century church, risking great harm to his physical body and even death. Today, life and culture are similar in the twenty-first Century as it was in the first century society. He suffered much persecution bringing the knowledge of the truth to the people of God concerning God's ultimate plan – beyond just being saved. That is, Christian life-living on the resurrection side of the cross; in which your relationship with Christ matures [character] – everything changes! (see 1 Corinthians 4:13).

The New Covenant and the Indwelling Spirit

At this point I want to again show you the need for the *indwelling power of the Holy Spirit*. And <u>I must emphasize again that no one in his or her *own strength* is able to live an overcoming life, free from sin's power and dominion.</u> He or she may grieve over their sins, cry a bucket of tears, but in their own *willpower* and *ability* they *cannot* defeat powerful, besetting sins.

When the prophet Ezekiel preached *repentance* to the nation of Israel, he knew that God was grieved over *Israel's backsliding and compromise.* He told the people:

> **"Repent, and turn from all your transgressions, so that iniquity will not be your ruin. Cast away from you all the transgressions which you have committed and get yourselves <u>a new heart and a new spirit</u> .... Therefore, turn and live!" (Ezekiel 18:30-32)**

In essence, Israel was being told, "You know what you are doing is wrong, so why don't you stop it? Lay it down. Just say no to your besetting sin. Turn from it and make a change in yourself – get yourself a new heart."

Ezekiel himself enjoyed the overcoming power of the Holy Spirit *in his life.* He was one of a number of Old Testament prophets whose holy lives were due <u>solely</u> to the indwelling presence of the Holy Spirit. All through Old Covenant times, we read of certain people who were touched by the Holy Spirit and filled with His presence.

The Holy Spirit Himself gave them the inner resources they needed to resist temptation and overcome sin. Though the Spirit had not been outpoured at this point, God in His mercy gave the Spirit to those who had been called to some great work. And it was the same with Ezekiel.

He experienced the power of the indwelling Holy Spirit. Listen to him testify, "The Spirit entered me when He spoke to me" (Ezekiel 2:2).

Ezekiel's present audience knew nothing of their need for the indwelling presence of God's Spirit. They could not overcome their sin no matter how hard they tried!

The same holds true for the church today in the individual Christian's life and corporately in the church. However, much of the church has rewritten the script [the Bible] to read just the opposite. It seems that every popular belief system coming along today believes you can just "Do it." "You don't have to take this stuff from the devil get mad and kick him out!" "You can break the chains yourself, just stop!" Does that sound familiar? I left home for the Army at eighteen, I loved God and had received Jesus as my Savior. I loved my parents and the Christian home they provided for us, but like Israel, no matter how hard I cried and tried I failed because all attempts were in my own strength. That struggle went on for years – until my wife finally got me to attend a small Pentecostal church with her while stationed in Kentucky and there I came into the knowledge of the truth. It grieves me today; the god of this world has hidden the truth today even from many in church leadership.

Throughout the years I had read many books which added to my burden of guilt and condemnation. I heard many convicting sermons. Under the New Covenant God demands total obedience. I wanted to "just do it." But I simply did not have the power within to accomplish it. Where can we find the power? The psalmist said, *"The secret of the LORD is with those who fear Him, and He will show them His covenant"* Psalm 24:14).

We now return to Ezekiel; he must have been really bent out of shape over what he saw going on in Israel. God's people were in disarray and the priests were focused on their own welfare and assembling all of the wealth for themselves. People wandered about everywhere looking for *spiritual food,* with no shepherds to feed them, lead them or bind their wounds.

Moreover, Scripture says, the Israelites were still living in sin and trusting in their own righteousness. God told Ezekiel, ***"They hear your words, but they do not do them; for with their mouth, they show much*** *love, but their hearts pursue their own gain ... They hear words, but they do not do them"* (Ezekiel 33:31-32).

During those dark days, God shared with Ezekiel a great mystery. God was about to unveil the New Covenant for him – and reveal to him a glorious work that would take place in the time of the Messiah. Suddenly the prophet's mouth was filled with words. Ezekiel began to preach a message as God spoke through him:

> *"Then I will sprinkle clean water on you, and you shall be clean; I will cleanse you from all your filthiness and from all your idols. I will give you <u>a new heart</u> and put a <u>new spirit</u> within you; I will take the heart of stone out of your flesh and give you a heart of flesh. <u>I will put My Spirit within you and cause you to walk in My statutes, and you will keep My judgments and do them"</u>* (Ezekiel 36:25-27).

Like the message of salvation today, this message was almost too good to be true. God was saying, "I am going to put My own Spirit in sinful people, and My Spirit will cause them to fulfill every command I have ever given them. They are dead to any ability to do in themselves. But My Spirit is going to empower them to turn away from their sin." Many of the Jews of old were convinced the Messiah would come to earth to set up a rich society for them, showering them with wealth, prosperity, and happiness without end. They thought Christ would give them all the world's resources and positions of power. So that they would not have to labor or strive anymore. Sadly, today some Christians expect this kind of kingdom.

God says, "The greatest blessing I can give sinners is free them from sin's grip through the blessing of My Son's ministry." An angel told Joseph in a dream that Mary would bear a son. And you shall call His name Jesus, for He will save His people from their sins" (Matthew 1:21). Being set free from the dominion of sin and its guilt is the greatest blessing he or she could have received. Praise God for He will conquer all my sins, by the inner working of the Holy Spirit. The apostolic ministers must walk in His New Covenant truth: Simply knowing that all my battles are not really mine – they are God's. Our part is simply to trust that He will do everything Christ sent Him to do. God has sworn by an oath to give us a new heart – one that is inclined to obey:

"I will give them a heart to know Me, that I am the LORD; and they shall be My people, and I will be their God for they shall return to Me with their whole heart" (Jeremiah 24:7). Again, He states: *"I will give you a new heart and put a new spirit within you ...."* (Ezekiel 36:26).

The same power that raised Jesus from the dead – and which enabled Him to fulfill God's Law through a perfect, sinless life now abides in us. God's own Spirit is alive in us, providing power over every work the enemy tries to bring against us. He promises to demolish all demonic strongholds. What is our part in all this? By faith we are to cast ourselves fully upon Him to lead us through every circumstance and situation. We must believe He will perform what He has promised. Give Him praise and glory!

Duties executed by the Apostolic

Apostolic ministers (Eph. 4:11), need to know the duties and functions of the apostolic in order to faithfully carry them out:

- The apostolic function is a ***gathering anointing***. Apostles gather people for the purpose of teaching, training and mobilizing them to fulfill the purposes and plans of God. They have the charisma to attract people for kingdom purposes. "He who is not with Me is against Me, and he who does not *gather* with Me scatters abroad" (Matthew 12:30). Italics added throughout.
- The apostolic anointing gives the ability to ***impart spiritual graces*** *to the saints,* which enables them to fulfill their callings and destinies (see Romans 1:11).
- The apostolic anointing gives the ability to ***stir up*** *and* ***mobilize*** the people of God to fulfill the Great Commission (Matthew 28:18-20).
- The apostolic anointing is a ***governing anointing*** necessary to facilitate the flow of God's power and anointing (see Titus 1:5).
- The apostolic anointing brings ***judgment*** and ***correction*** to the church. They bring verdicts against false teaching and incorrect behavior.

- The apostolic anointing brings the *necessary change* to the house of God – during times of reformation (see Hebrews 9:10).
- The apostolic anointing is a master builder, anointed to help *build strong churches.* They are responsible for overseeing the construction.
- The apostolic anointing help *establish truth, revelation, churches* and new moves of the Spirit.
- The apostolic anointing works through spiritual fathers and mothers. As they *birth, protect, teach,* and *mentor.* They restore the principle of father and motherhood to the church.
- The apostolic anointing has a unique ability *to execute the plans and purposes of God.* They execute means to carry out, perform or do. This anointing is absolutely necessary to fulfill the Great Commission.
- The apostolic anointing *defends the faith.* They *defend the truth.* They *defend the church* from outside attacks and infiltration by the enemy (see Philippians 1:17).
- The apostolic anointing *trains* and *educates* ministers. They develop leadership.
- The apostolic anointing *ordains* and *set-in place* qualified leadership (see Titus 1:5). The apostolic ordination releases *fruitfulness* (see John 15:16).
- The apostolic anointing *confronts false teaching, witchcraft, immorality,* anything that will keep the church from fulfilling its purpose.
- The apostolic anointing is a *confrontational anointing* (see Galatians 2:11).
- The apostolic anointing is *focused on finishing* (see John 4:34).

When the apostolic minister faithfully executes his or her duties, the people *birthed* into the Kingdom and *discipled* into the Kingdom by his or her ministry will be faithful "epistles" to all men – reflecting the apostolic dimension rising in a manner that they will be effective in the ministries to which God has called them.

SECTION IV

APOSTOLIC TIMES

(SERVICE)

CHAPTER TEN

A FUNCTIONING APOSTOLIC COMMUNITY

"But speaking the truth in love, may grow up in all things into him who is the head – Christ – from whom the whole body, joined and knit together by what every joint supplies according to the effective working by which every part does its share, causes growth of the body for the edifying of itself in love" (Ephesians 4:15-16).

During my many years as a leader in the military, I came to recognize and appreciate quality assurance [personnel], to the point of implementing the function in some form in all of my leadership positions during my 26.5 years army career. Those persons holding this position must be individuals of outstanding integrity, character, humility, trust, and technical expertise. These individuals on numerous occasions are required to communicate and advise through delegated authority major commanders on the outside of the chain of command, who in turn speak authoritatively with their leaders up the chain of command. The objective being "truth."

Honesty and truth are of the utmost importance – sometimes requiring a mission "stand down" or "stop to all operations" of the unit to make necessary strategic and tactical changes, in policy, equipment and training in order to be relevant and "ready" to meet any contingency that may arise. Now with all the above in the world. It is imperative that the apostolic minister ensure these same dedicated qualities are executed within the local churches.

Why not the Church?

"God chose us "in Christ" before the foundation of the world, that we should be blameless and holy before Him" (see Ephesians 11:4). We can see very clearly that the church is no afterthought with God. It was planned long before the world was formed. He is not, *first* of all, as concerned with what a church *does* – as with what the church *is*.

Being must always precede *doing*, for what we *are* determines what we *do*.

To understand the *moral character* of God's people is essential to understand the nature of the church. As Christians, we are to be *moral examples* to the world, reflecting the pure *character* and *holiness* of Jesus Christ. Christ has built in quality assurance through the Holy Spirit's enablement and guidance, the Bible and the apostolic leadership ministries within the body of Christ (Ephesians 4:11). Many churches today have lost their corporate identity. This causes many Christians to think they stand alone, before God and that they are not accountable to anyone else, including their local church. But the church is the body of Christ, and it functions best when all its members are ready and able "to serve" and "to share."

It is *imperative* that all know what God wants His church to be and to do. Therefore, as part of His body, God calls the church to reveal to the world the glory of His character, which is found in the face of Jesus Christ. This is restated in chapter 1 of Ephesians. "He has put all things under His [Christ's] feet and has made Him the head over all things for the church, which is His body, the fullness of Him who fills all in all" (Ephesians 1:22-23).

Paul says that all that Jesus Christ is (His fullness) is to be seen in His body – which is the church! The message of the church to the world is to declare Him, to talk about Jesus Christ. The presentation of the gospel for Christ today remains God's strategy today for soul winning. Notice Acts 2:41 and 2 Timothy 2:2 respectively and their results:

"Then those who gladly received his word were baptized; and that day about three thousand souls were added to them."

"And the things that you have heard from me among many witnesses, commit these to faithful men who will be able to teach others also."

The church then is God's redemptive agent in the world. He has a purpose for the church therefore, He places every member in a church to accomplish his redemptive purposes. "So then, you are no longer strangers and sojourners, but you are fellow citizens with the saints and members of the household of God, built upon the foundation of the apostles and prophets. Christ Jesus Himself being the chief cornerstone, in whom the whole structure is joined together and grows into a holy temple in the Lord: in whom you also are built into it for a dwelling place of God in the Spirit" (Ephesians 2:19-22).

Truly these verses make it perfectly clear as the Lord Jesus Himself confirms this calling in the opening chapter of the book of Acts. Just before Jesus ascended to His Father, He said to His disciples: "You shall receive power when the Holy Spirit has come upon you; and you shall be My witnesses in Jerusalem and in all Judea and Samaria and to the end of the earth" (Acts 1:8).

The church is called to be a witness – and a witness is one who declares and demonstrates. Listen to the apostle Peter's wonderful word about the churches witnessing role in his first letter: "You are a chosen race, a royal priesthood, a holy nation, God's own people, that you may declare the wonderful deeds of Him who called you out of darkness into His marvelous light" (1 Peter 2:9).

As stated earlier, the responsibility to fulfill this calling belongs to all true Christians – all are indwelt by the Holy Spirit, all are expected to fulfill their calling in the midst of the world. Here a problem appears, the problem of counterfeit Christians. It is easy for the individual Christian or the church corporately to talk about displaying the character and to make great claims about doing so. However, as many knowledgeable unbelievers know from close observation, the image many Christians project is not always the true, biblical image of Jesus Christ.

The church cannot save the world – but
the Lord of the church can.

That is why Paul is so careful to describe authentic Christlike character: "With all lowliness and meekness, with patience, forbearing one another in love, eager to maintain the unity of the Spirit in the bond of peace" (Ephesians 4:2-3).

The post-ascension apostolic

There is an old African proverb that says, "He who goes alone, goes faster; but those who go together, go farther." In this section I would like to share with you a pertinent reason why the apostolic church is a gift from God: that together as the body of Christ we can go farther and accomplish far more than we could ever do on our own as individuals. The apostolic church is an organism[10] not an organization[11]. The church is the living and moving body of Christ designed by God as a means of multiplying the salvation experience to those in need (see 2 Timothy 2:2).

When we all come together and each person gives their time, gifts, and finances as moved by the Spirit, there is certainly a greater *quantity* and *quality assurance* of people and resources available to do kingdom work. A great example of this happened when the early church in Jerusalem suffered during a major famine.

Paul went to the churches he had planted and asked them to save up money to assist their fellow Christians in Jerusalem (see 1 Corinthians 16:1-2; 2 Corinthians 8-9). These funds provided

---

[10] Organism – an individual living thing as a person, animal, or plant. Webster's New Explorer Dictionary and Thesaurus (Merriam – Webster Inc. 1999) 369

[11] Organization – the act or process of organizing or being organized. An administrative structure to join in a union. Ibid. Page 369

by believers living in Corinth, Galatia, and Philippi were able to do more quantitatively by pooling their resources together to serve their fellow Christians in Christ. It is important to note these were Gentile churches foundationally planted by the apostle to the Gentiles, Paul. Two thousand years later, if Paul were still alive, he would probably still be defending his apostleship.

The Book of Act

The Book of Acts is a historical narrative providing a condensed witness of the early church. A believer's faith rests upon the facts of history: the life, death, and resurrection of Jesus Christ. Luke recorded these historical events in his Gospel in order to invoke *belief*. If the historical fact of Christ's resurrection is not true – then a believer's faith has no foundation. As Paul states, *"If Christ is not risen, your faith is futile; you are still in your sins"* (1 Corinthians 15:17). This book reassures believers that their faith in Christ rests on facts. The extraordinary growth of the early church was based directly on the resurrected Christ. His command, and empowerment, and deployment of the disciples through the power of Holy Spirit is the only reasonable explanation for the incredible spread of the gospel in the first century. The early Christians were not testifying about a dead Christ, but a living Christ whom they had seen with their own eyes (see Acts 1:1-5; Luke 24:36-53; 2 Peter 1:16). The same is true for us today! Jesus lives and continues to work through the church as evidenced by the Holy Spirit's presence and supernatural power (see Acts 1:8).

Looking at the powerless condition many local churches find themselves in today, it is quite evident that they have either denied the Holy Spirit, His gifts and ministries and settled for a "bloodless" institutional religion, or they have just let secular society convince them that He is not here as Jesus promised He would be. Undoubtedly, these churches are led by people with a different agenda. Therefore, *their* corrupt theology categorizes the Holy Spirit along with the apostles, prophets, and teachers (see Acts 13:10) as: "obsolete," or "no longer necessary?" God forbid! Let there be no doubt, those who are His know that Bible standards and the Spiritual Church of the Living God are unchanged. Christ is very much alive and thriving by His Spirit in His true saints!

Paul's Example

Just as with Eve in the beginning, Satan continues to try and get the people of God to change the Word of God to mean something else. Repeat a lie long enough and it will become truth (to you). After the ascension according to Ephesians 4:11, the apostolic ministries [apostles, prophets, evangelists, pastors, and teachers] are to be *functioning* parts of the body of Christ given by Christ Himself to build up and equip Christians to full maturity – throughout the church age:

> *"till we all come to the unity of the faith and the knowledge of the Son of God, to a perfect man, to the measure of the stature of the fulness of Christ"*(Ephesians 4:13).

The apostle Paul belonged to that ministry – as he was met on the road to Damascus by the *ascended* Jesus who called him to be the apostle to the Gentiles. In addition to His call, Paul had some outstanding credentials in the world, yet he still must graduate from God's school of the Spirit before he was ready to be sent into his calling. And though Paul had the Word of God and a vision implanted in his heart, the people seemed to question his motivation for ministry. When you read his testimony, it may hit you that he had an element of pride in him. However, a study of the life of Paul reveals after spending 10-13 years in seclusion he ultimately gave God glory for the work of grace in his life (see 2 Corinthians 11:16-33; Philippians 3:5-7).

In any case, preparation to be an effective ministry for the Lord involves much more than an education. It involves being emptied of pride and other self-ambitions – that would get in the way of fruitful ministry for God. All we know is when God was through with Paul, he was fit for the master's service. With his finished motive he could say to the Ephesian elders:

> *"I have coveted no one's silver or gold or apparel. Yes, you yourselves know that these hands have provided for my necessities, and for those who were with me. I have shown you in every way, by laboring like this, that you must support the weak. And remember the words of the Lord Jesus, that He said, "It is more blessed to give than to receive"* (Acts 20:33-35).

And then to the Thessalonians:

> *"For our exhortation did not come from error or uncleanness, nor was it in deceit. But as we have been approved by God to be entrusted with the gospel, even as we speak, not as pleasing men, but God who tests our hearts. For neither at any time did we use flattering words, as you know, nor a cloak for covetousness – God is witness. Nor did we seek glory from men, either from you or from others, when we might have made demands as apostles of Christ. But we were gentle among you, first as a nursing mother cherishes her own children"* (2 Thessalonians 2:3-7).

Paul may have been forgotten by men, but God never forgot him. While others doubted God laid Paul on the heart of Barnabas who after a few years with him laid the spiritual foundation for the church at Antioch through his teaching. Actually, it was due to Paul's persecution of the church earlier when he was Saul of Tarsus, that the church at Antioch was established by believers scattered from Jerusalem who fled to other areas of the region to escape Paul's grasp. Under Barnabas, Paul had a great opportunity to hone his gifts and develop his teaching skills. Soon Barnabas and Paul had *reproduced themselves in others.* It was first at Antioch that believers were called Christians. This church had grown strong with other prophets and teachers (see Acts 13:1).

After a special time of fasting and prayer and waiting on God, the Holy Spirit said, *"Now separate to Me Barnabas and Saul for the work to which I have called them."* Then, having fasted and prayed, and laid hands on them, they **sent** them away (Acts 13:1-3).

To serve this present Age

Paul had been called to be an apostle as a young man (probably 30 years old), now many years later he was to be a **"sent one"** (apostle), about 45 years old. Once sent, over a period of 20 years, Paul traveled to more than 100 cities and preached in about 30 of them. He planted at least 10 strong, reproducing churches.

It is important to make a distinction between these different categories of apostolic ministry and separate Paul from the twelve. Paul serves as our example for apostolic ministry today. Many through the centuries have insisted that apostles and prophets are longer needed in the church. That is one way to shun having to personally explain why we do not experience the Bible standard. Actually, it should drive us to seek God for the truth. To some they will cease when *"that which is perfect has come"* (1 Corinthians 13:10). The Greek word for perfect means "end" or "completion." Biblical scholars seem to lean toward one of two interpretations: **1)** There is probably reference to Christ's Second Coming and the finish of all things (see v. 12). **2)** The other interprets perfect as referring to the completion of the New Testament. If we use the rule of interpretation, to let the clear passages interpret the unclear passages. Ephesians 4 clearly tells us the time frame for the apostolic ministries and what the "perfect" is too be. These ministries are given by Christ, *"till we all come to the unity of the faith and of the knowledge of the Son of God, to a perfect man, to the measure of the stature of the fullness of Christ"* (Ephesians 4:13). I do not believe this passage has reached fruition yet.

The purpose of the apostolic

If the Word of God says the apostolic ministries are to continue until Christ's returns – once the COVID-19 pandemic is over if it is the Lord's will, it will end soon. We must stop talking and debating which side is right and turn our focus to how the apostolic ministries *function* – the true biblical application of the ministries for the last Days – to complete the Great Commission. Christ Himself gave some:

Apostles – the first position (the Generals) of church leadership is the office of the apostle. Some say there were no apostles after the original twelve. But there are at least twenty-four apostles mentioned in the New Testament alone, and I know apostles are in the church today. In fact, as long as there is a church, there will be apostles. I know people today with apostolic ministries – people around the world who are doing the work of an apostle at this very moment, and I believe there will be many more. In these last days, the greatest ministries are going to become greatly accelerated along with the operation and functions of the Holy Spirit. An apostle is not appointed by man. The Bible says the Holy Spirit establishes these ministries or functions in the church. Apostles are born through the power of the Holy Spirit. The apostle is different than the other four apostolic ministries in that he or she has the ability to perform those *other* functions. This is why the apostle is always listed in the Bible first. Some think the prophet should be listed first.

The apostle is above the prophet. Any person man or woman with the apostolic calling has the ability, the authority, and the anointing to raise up a church without any outside help. We have three apostles within the Bread of Life Ministries, who have done just that, and have birthed four additional churches.

Paul had this ability. He could go into a town, walk into the marketplace and teach the truth of God's Word and have a church formed in a matter of days. Not only could he raise up a church, but he also had the power and ability to remain there as pastor. He could teach the people in the church, then start a school and send out apostolic workers to other places. The apostle is a *combination* of the other apostolic church functions – as the twenty-four NT apostles mentioned above. You may be surprised to know that the first one is **the Lord Jesus Christ.** Hebrews 3:1 says,

> *Wherefore, holy brethren, partakers of the heavenly calling, consider the Apostle and High Priest of our profession, Christ Jesus.*

Jesus was Heaven sent: *"God so loved the world, that He gave* [sent] *His only begotten Son* ......[the Lord Jesus Christ]*"* (John 3:16).

The office of apostle involves the total ministry of God, and Christ had a total ministry. He no doubt was the most complete apostle the world has ever known – all of what it means to be a "sent one." Jesus always said, to do what He was told to do of the Father.

Paul is the model for the New Testament apostles, prophets, evangelists, pastors, and teachers. In Galatians 1:1 in establishing his apostleship we read,

> *Paul, an apostle, (not of men, neither by men, but of Jesus Christ, and God the Father, who raised him from the dead).*

Paul was saying to all, "I am Paul, an apostle." Here he was defining his relationship with the body of Christ, which you can accept or reject. If the Holy Spirit appointed Paul to this job, he was speaking by the anointing of the Holy Spirit – undoubtedly what he said was true. Also, in Galatians we read what Paul wrote about Peter: *"For he that wrought effectually in Peter to the apostleship of the circumcision, the same was mighty in me toward the Gentiles"* (Galatians 2:8). Paul was showing how Peter had become an apostle to a certain group, the circumcision (the Jews). I have seen this Spirit-directed apostleship demonstrated. An apostle of God [today] has an ability and a ministry, but he or she *must be* directed to where God wants them.

Apostles are the leaders God has commissioned to lead His church. An apostle is one who can be a pioneer or reformer, who can construct and begin a work with no problem. Not only can he or she conceive and bring into being a body of believers, but they can also remain and found that church putting it on a solid foundation of truth. The apostle can organize it, set it in order, and teach it with accuracy of the truth. The new apostolic rising will have to re-think and re-examine the Scriptures to discover and receive instructions from the Holy Spirit on how to build the house of God differently than what we see around us today.

Some called to this ministry do not use the title apostle – however, they perform the same functions as others who are called by God to the office and placed in the body of Christ by the Holy Spirit. The new apostolic rising will recover and restore what has been lost throughout the centuries concerning church leadership. In order to do this, we will see:

- denominations falling.
- One-man ministries that have enslaved the church for centuries will fail and fold up.
- Pride, egos, arrogance, control and manipulation will be broken.
- Preeminence will not find a place.

The Spirit is saying to church leaders in the earth right now – to stop building God's house around one-man or one-woman ministries and start building to the pattern found in the New Testament. The NT pattern calls for a plurality of *elders* giving leadership to a body of believers by an apostle who planted the church. In every church founded in the New Testament, there were multiple elders who gave shared oversight of the flock.

There was never one man or woman that called all the shots, had unilateral authority, and answered *to no one*. The Scripture speaks of *ministers* (plural). Once the church was planted by an apostle and proper foundation was laid, the oversight and daily affairs were handed over to a plurality of elders who governed the church together as a team. I will list some Scriptures to support this:

- Elder(s) governed the church at Jerusalem (Acts 15).
- Elder(s) are found in the churches of Judea and the surrounding area (Acts 11:30; James 5:14,15).
- A plurality of Elder(s) was established in the churches of Derbe, Lystra, Iconium, and Antioch (Acts 14:23; in the church at Ephesus (Acts 20:17; 1 Timothy3:1-7; 5:17-25); in the church at (Philippi (Philippians 1:1); and in the churches on the island of Crete (Titus 1:5).
- According to 1 Peter, a plurality of elder(s) existed in churches throughout northwestern Asia minor: Pontus, Galatia, Cappadocia, Asia, and Bithynia (1 Peter 1:1; 5:1). We will have more to say about the elders later, I mentioned them in this section, because of their close proximity with the apostle. **Apostles reproduce themselves.**
- All those who have a place of apostolic leadership in Christ Jesus will suffer persecution – Satan, the prince of this world will see to that.

Prophets – the second ministerial office is that of the prophet. The prophet foretells God's actions in the future. God has used prophets and prophetesses throughout the Bible, and He wants to do the same today in an even greater way. God in these last days, wants to breathe upon the total church of the Lord Jesus Christ and speak to us through these dedicated and anointed vessels, that we might know things that will surely come to pass and that we might have direction. God does have prophets and prophetesses today; He is speaking to people – but much of the body of Christ is ignorant of this fact and not desirous of it. Two things keep us from knowing that: sin and unbelief. Unbelief cuts off the miracle working power of God. Let the prophetic voice be heard throughout the land. **Prophets reproduce themselves.**

Evangelists – the office of an evangelist is to proclaim the Gospel of Jesus Christ. The evangelist is a gift from God to the church who help bring people into the body of Christ, by presenting Christ's love and forgiveness and offering the free salvation by grace through faith. They train others to do the same (see 2 Timothy 2:2). **Evangelists reproduce themselves.**

Pastors – the office of pastor is a shepherd. The Greek word *poimen* is used seventeen times in the New Testament. Only one time, in Ephesians 4:11 is it translated "pastor." So, Paul was saying that the pastor is to be the shepherd of his or her flock, the local church. The pastor does for the church what a shepherd does for the sheep the outcome demonstrates the pastor's heart, to feed the flock with knowledge and understanding, nurtures, cares for and protects from the enemy. Jesus is the Chief Shepherd, the Chief Pastor. He saw the multitudes and was moved with compassion (see Matthew 9:36). In. addition to the shepherd, the Word of God speaks of hirelings – people who say they are pastors but are not (John 10:11-13).

There is a vast difference between a person who is hired to be a pastor and one who has been commissioned by God to do the work, even if never paid. The distinguishing mark is the *pastor's heart*. **Pastors reproduce themselves.**

Teachers – the office of a teacher is a ministerial office and carries an incredibly special anointing for opening people's understanding of the truth of God's Word. All of the available education in the world will not make a teacher of God's Word. A teacher is a person who has been set in the body of Christ by God for one specific purpose: *to teach truth*. Additionally, one may observe that in all three main passages listing the gifts of the Spirit, *teaching* is listed (see Ephesians 4:11; 1 Cor.12:12; Romans 12:4-5).

Therefore, the teaching gift and the teachers
who have it become critical elements in the
building up of the Body of Christ through the
exposition of the Word, the single message.

I was amazed at the number of great Bible teachers who were almost illiterate. I met a couple of these teachers as a young teenager traveling to various churches and conferences with my father, who was a pastor.

Oh! But when these men and women gave an exposition on the Word of God, they were powerfully anointed to teach the truth of the Word!

The spiritual gift of teaching is given to some believers anointed and empowered by the Holy Spirit to serve the local church and or the church at large with a clear presentation of the body of truth which is the "faith." Therefore, both the individual and the corporate body can apply the truth to their respective "lives," perform the work of the ministry, and advance toward their goals given for them in the Great Commission.

I have been teaching the Word of God for more than forty-five years and I will never forget that early-on basic training and example I received from those old masters (old wineskins). The anointing breaks the yoke! **Teachers reproduce themselves.**

The apostolic restoration

It is imperative that all five apostolic *ministers'* functions are for the equipping of the saints for the:

1) work of ministry,
2) for the edifying of the body of Christ,
3) till we all come to the unity of the faith,
4) and the knowledge of the Son of God,
5) to a perfect man,
6) to the measure of the stature of the fulness of Christ.
7) Reproducing themselves.

That we should no longer be children, tossed to and fro and carried about with every wind of doctrine, by the trickery of men, in the cunning craftiness of deceitful plotting, but speaking **the truth in love,** may grow up in all things into Him who is the head – Christ – from whom the whole body, joined and knit together by what every joint supplies, according to the effective working by which every part does its share, causes growth of the body for the edifying of itself *in love* (1 Corinthians 4:14-16).

Although we witness many abuses of these titles by those who claim to be authentic and are not. we must release ourselves to the body of Christ. This would mean to spiritual things like deliverance, healing, miracles, and all the supernatural gifts of the Holy Spirit. This applies to all of the ministries described in the Book of Acts.

Truly these signs do follow those
who believe these signs!

The counterfeits must be countered! I feel that today is the *day* of the saints – the COVET-19 pandemic has really challenged the saints to the task. I am not speaking of the institutional church hierarchy – but all regular anointed Christians on the front lines in intercessory prayers.

People are calling on the Lord as the situations are really worsening. The churches having been declared "non-essential" by science and government, in many cases, it is left up to the family members and strangers to minister to their sick, comfort their families and bury their dead, with death all around them – but a day of the saints is wherever they are found! Is all of this a "wake up call" for the church to return to her [call], the Great Commission!

Christians among the ranks of first responders, doctors, nurses, hospital workers, emergency rescue teams, police, bus and truck drivers, and other services have many opportunities to minister to those around them. In spite of what is reported in the news media many people have repented of their sins and have come to Christ for salvation, others have renewed their personal commitment to the Lord, and many are calling on Him for the first time. All of us who remain should rejoice and be thankful that by God's grace and mercy we are still here. Perhaps we should ask the question, why?

One reason we are still here is to continue the Lord's assigned work. What was deemed non-essential by man was the church buildings – not the body of Christ (Church). If we never *(fully)* assemble in those church buildings again, we still have the duties assigned to us in the Great Commission (see Matthew 28:19-20).

The first church "turned the world upside down" – assembling together in their houses, on porches, in gardens, caves, deserts, deep woods, streets, fields, and vineyards. Church through "teams" ministry works [prayer, study, praise, and worship]. It is time to revive our personal and corporate prayer ministries not only because of COVID-19, but for the sake of the weakened church in America, and our national and local leadership. Satan has stepped up his game knowing that his time is short! Today, along with changing the word of God, he is establishing "THE LIE" (prayerfully study Romans 1:18-25).

Each day presents wonderful opportunities to express Christ's love to others. As I expressed earlier, "only good can overcome evil!" The late Dr. Billy Graham's research discovered that about 90% of Christians in America were living defeated spiritual lives according to Scripture.

Your testimony

Many people are posting their story on social media and daily adding to it. A few are sharing their testimony (what has the Lord done or is doing [supernaturally] in their personal life lately)? Something that only God can do! The Scripture says, "God *sent* His Word" to Heal. His Word heals, praise God. There's strength in talking about Jesus! Tell it! My purpose in writing this book is to encourage your heart by sharing some things that God is doing in this country and the whole world [that He so loves] in this period of time called the Last Days. He is so Wonderful!

Though, Satan has devised a masterful deceptive plan with the intent to keep us from walking and talking in the power of the Holy Spirit – according to the Scriptures, and he is experiencing far too much victory in the personal lives of Christians and in our local Christian churches. **Saints reproduce themselves.**

Deception is a dangerous thing! It is determined by the *fruit* produced from one's actions as compared to the teachings found in the Word of God. The fruit produced in our *society* by the *body of Christ* in recent years reflect the truth of our success toward deception. Why? The answer is found in the Word of God, *"My people are destroyed [defeated] for a lack of knowledge"* (Hosea 4:6). Study the Word, watch, and pray let the Spirit give you a personal word of truth to counter Satan's LIE!

Finding a Christian who has a fear of
sinning today is rare today!

Society has developed an overpowering ability to influence and teach us its humanistic values, standards, secular worldview and hedonistic lifestyles. Prophetic Scriptures **warn** that we are living in one of the most difficult periods as righteous standards in this country in recent years has passed the point where God's values are no longer the major influence in everyday life.

When I was growing up, a large portion of the congregation considered themselves to be Christian, because they were water-baptized, and attended church regularly. But when it came to faith and doctrine, these cultural Christians really did not buy into the Bible. Today, most of their descendants just see those things as irrelevant. People who were not Christians no longer claim to be. Many find this change from these social norms refreshing.

Our culture is so focused on materialism and convenience, which prevents many people from committing to all God has for the church in this season. These mindsets cannot be broken by education only, but these truths must be fleshed out. Then only through the power of the Holy Spirit, not by might, nor by power, but by the Holy Spirit. Satan can overcome our flesh in a snap.

I believe unless a person *experiences* the person and the power of the Holy Spirit[12] there can be *no* transformation. Satan has loosed his heavy weights upon this nation, seducing and deceiving spirits of religion and rationalization that tempt God's people to:

- To exchange the truth of God's Word for that which is totally contrary to the Word of God.
- To make something wrong seem innocent and irresistible.
- To make the difference between black and white seem like a shade of gray. There is no middle ground between truth and a lie.
- To serve our own interests above our desire to please God; and we put our standards before God's.
- To call those things that are wrong – right; and call those things that are right – wrong.

I repeat, if we do not know the Word of God and diligently seek righteousness and hate what God hates, we will become easy prey to these deceiving spirits. But what if we communicated to all church members that Jesus has elevated, having *love* for our neighbors to the level of the second commandment, superseded only by the command to love God?

The church is all of God's people in ministry sharing the Gospel with people of *all* nations. The church is reborn flesh-and-blood people who are God's *ministers* of reconciliation (2 Corinthians 5:17-21). Again,

---

[12] Acts 1:8

the church is a living organism. All of God's people belong to the New testament *"ministerium."* The word "minister" is usually equated with "clergy." It is *not* so in the Bible. In Scripture it is linked to the Greek word *diakonia.* this may be translated *"service"* or *"ministry."* And is by no means restricted to what a pastor does in a church building.

The Holy Spirit's gifts and fruit of the Spirit

Spiritual gifts are extraordinary divine enablement(s) for ministry that the Holy Spirit gives in some measure to all believers and are to be completely under His control and used *for building up the church to Christ's glory*. Even though such attributes as faith, teaching, and giving are considered spiritual gifts, *all* Christians are exhorted to develop these three common traits.

There are no other doctrines as important to the world scene today as the apostolic restoration and operation of the fruit of the Spirit and the gifts of the Spirit in the body of Christ. Our outlook and practice both individually and corporately will have a definite bearing on our final rewards.

The Scripture tells us, *"for the earnest expectation of the creature waiteth for the **manifestation** of the **sons of God"*** (Romans 8:19). KJV There will be a day when the sons of God will ultimately become manifest. Certainly, all professed Christians are expecting to be included, but unfortunately most are *passively* awaiting His arrival. Those who are *expectantly awaiting* Christ's arrival will obviously be manifested. According to the passage above it is the sons of God who will receive manifestation.

In the Greek, this particular word for sons
is *huios,* a word which emphasizes the *personal
relationship* of an offspring to its parent – especially
the *character* or *nature* of that parent.[13]

---

[13] Vine's Complete Expository of the Old and New Testament (Thomas Nelson Inc Nashville, 1985) 585

Here Paul uses it to refer to the relationship of the children *born into the family of God. [their heavenly Father].* These children will be manifest or recognized by their Christ-like character (again see Galatians 5:22,23).

Sadly, many people who are saved, and baptized in the Holy Spirit – have *never developed* an intimate personal relationship with their heavenly Father. The Apostle John wrote, *"But as many as received Him, to them gave He the <u>power to become</u> the sons of God even to them that believe on His name: Which were born, not of blood, nor of the will of the flesh, nor of the will of man, but of God* (John 1:12, 13). The Greek word for *sons* in John 1:12 in the Greek is not *huios* but *teknon.*

> This Greek word *teknon* emphasizes the *fact of birth* rather than the *character* of their heavenly Father, and the fact that this person has *never* developed a personal relationship with Him.[14]

This explains Dr. Billy Graham's conclusion referred to earlier concerning those who have never developed a personal relationship with the heavenly Father. Sadly, our local churches are full of such Christians – they are content just being in the family of God serving *collectively* with their brothers and sisters in the Lord – whether as an usher, teaching a Sunday school class or just tithing and attending. The question is, are they manifested as the sons of God? Is their Christianity "vain" because they have never developed a personal relationship with the heavenly Father? Their religion never reveals God's character/ nature to the world.

Time will tell

In the early 70's, I had a dream of a man running in the desert kicking up a great cloud of dust. The enormous cloud spread up and out behind him as if it would totally consume him way down at the bottom – he seemed to be running for his life, but he was never overcome by the cloud. I pondered that dream through the years. One day in 1980 while sitting my office at U.S. Army Movement Control Headquarters, just

---

[14] Ibid. 585

off the main lobby of the main train station in Seoul, South Korea – an Englishman walked in and introduced himself to me as Keith Shaw, a missionary from London, England, as we chatted, he told me that he had just arrived in the city from the country of Bahrain where he was a missionary. Certainly, I was interested in hearing him, he said God sent him to Korea for He had a black man there that he was to help with the deeper truths of God's Word. The Holy Spirit moved right there in that office [we conversed for several hours] as we prayerfully confirmed the fact that I was that black man that Brother Shaw was seeking. I took him home with me that evening and introduced him to my wife and children, then we got him settled in for the night. The next day he accompanied me to my office. I introduced him to my boss and other staff members there in the Headquarters. Brother Shaw and I were almost inseparable during the next year. We spent numerous hours in the Word when I was off duty and on weekends. I shared the dream with him. He interpreted it to me: What I saw as dust was really thousands of people following the little man (me) running way down at the base of the dust storm. I had accepted my call into the gospel ministry six months prior to Brother Shaw's visit, however, I was called to teach the truths of God's Word ten years earlier. One day just as mysteriously as he appeared that morning in the train station – he was gone.

My family and I returned to the United States and Fort Bragg, North Carolina where I retired on July 1, 1984. Then came three years of Bible College, graduate school and 38 years of pastoral ministry which includes several solid church plants and 1 Bible college and church plant and 22 years later all are still thriving to the glory of God. The Lord has been gracious, and we give Him all the honor, praise and glory. I am now 80 years old and my wife is 76 and we are still running for Jesus. We are all in the midst of this COVID-19 epidemic and God is still blessing. God sent Evangelist Tommy Burns and his wife Donna to us with enough tech-savvy to project the Bread of Life Ministries to thousands around the world twice weekly – this addition came just before the epidemic struck. The dream is coming to fruition. Praise God. Today my wife and I are trusting God and training/ mentoring those who will replace us and carry on the Bread of Life apostolic vision for the Kingdom of God!

Some who walked with us in the founding years including our first president of the Bread of Life Bible Institute, Dr. J.C. Williams left us (Oct. 2006) to be with the Lord. We are thankful for others who are still here, still praying, and still supporting the Bread of Life. The 70's dream is bearing much fruit. To GOD be the Glory!

> *"Now you are the body of Christ, and members individually. And God has appointed these in the church: first apostles, second prophets, third teachers, after that miracles, then gifts of healings, helps, administrations, varieties of tongues. Are all apostles? Are all prophets? Are all teachers? Are all workers of miracles? Do all have gifts of healings? Do all speak with tongues? Do all interpret? But earnestly desire the best gifts. And yet I show you a more excellent way"* (1 Corinthians 12:27-31).

The answer to each of the questions is emphatically, NO! Then, the apostle Paul uses an exaggeration to illustrate the *uselessness* of each spiritual gift *without love:*

> *Though I speak with the tongues of men and of angels, but have not love, I have become as sounding brass or a clanging cymbal. And though I have the gift of prophecy, and understand all mysteries and all knowledge, and though I have all faith, so that I could remove mountains, but have not love, I am nothing. And though I bestow all my goods to feed the poor, and though I give my body to be burned, but have not love, it profits me nothing* (1Cor.13:1-3).

Paul made it noticeably clear without love, what you produce when you try to function in the true gifts of the Spirit is not complete. Then verse 13 says, *"And now abide faith, hope, love, these three; but the greatest of these is love."*

The first work – developing the character of Christ

Love and obedience are inseparable and are manifested in us through the *fruit* produced by God in the transforming, regenerating power of the Holy Spirit. God has implanted within our hearts evidence that we belong to Him in that we love Him, the One who first loved us (see Romans 5:5).

The Greek term is "agape" meaning sacrificial, unconditional love. This love is manifested through His glorious Presence in each true believer. This is crucial for the apostolic anointing to function. In I

Corinthians 13 sandwiched between chapters 12 where the of Spiritual gifts are listed and chapter 14 where the operations of the gifts are explained is Chapter 13 called the love chapter; where we are told "the greatest of these is love." The apostolic gifts of the Spirit can operate properly only through the love of God shed abroad in the hearts of the children of God – to the world.

We can reach out to save the world in which we live today, but it will never happen through organizational strength, numbers, or gimmicks. With a few, God can win the battle and mightily take care of thousands of the enemy (see Judges 7 and 8). Likewise, doing apostolic ministry God's way by His Spirit can equal an incalculable result. Thus, being led by the Spirit, is twofold:

- First, we must receive instructions from God.
- Secondly, we must fulfill God's will in the Spirit (character) of Jesus.

It bears repeating over and over again, God desires that the *character* of his individual children undergo a transformational process becoming identical with the character of Jesus. In Romans 8:29, the Apostle Paul states,

> *"For whom He did foreknow, He also did predestinate to be conformed to the image of His Son, that he might be the firstborn among many brethren."*

Being conformed to the image of Jesus simply means taking on His form, His likeness, and His stature or image. Developing the character of Jesus is accomplished by developing the same fruit that were easily recognized in His life. Jesus Himself taught in Matthew 7:15,16,20, that it is by outward manifestation of [fruit] that inward nature [character] is recognized not only by believers but it is also by their fruit that the world recognizes them. When Jesus in essence said, *"You shall recognize My disciples by their character."* The fruit of the Spirit consists of nine character-building Christ-like traits spoken of in Galatians 5:22,23:

1) **Love** – the Greek term is "agape" meaning unconditional love. This love is not referring to emotional affections, physical attractions, or familial bonds – but to respect, devotion, and

affection that lead to willing service (see John 15:13; Romans 5:8; John 3:16,17).

2) **Joy** – is happiness based on unchanging divine promises and kingdom realities. It is the sense of well-being experienced by one who knows all is well in spite of favorable or non-favorable life circumstances (see John 16:20-22).

3) **Peace** – is the inner calm that results from confidence in a saving relationship with Christ. Like joy, peace is not related to one's circumstances of life (see John 14:27; Romans 8:28; Philippians 4:6-7,9).

4) **Longsuffering** – refers to the ability to endure persecution, injuries inflicted by others and the willingness to accept irritating or painful people and situations (see Ephesians 4:2; Colossians 3:12; 1 Timothy 1:15-16).

5) **Kindness** – is tender concern for others, reflected in a desire to treat others gently, just as Christ treats all true believers (see Matthew 11:28-29; 19:13-14; 2 Timothy 2:24).

6) **Goodness** – is moral and spiritual excellence manifested in active kindness (see Romans 5:7; 6:10; 2 Thessalonians 1:11).

7) **Faithfulness** – is loyalty and trustworthiness (see Lamentations 3:22; Philippians 2:7-9; 1Thessalonians 5:24; Revelation 2:10).

8) **Gentleness** – also translated "meekness" is a humble and gentle attitude that is patiently submissive in every offense, while having no desire for revenge or retribution (see Galatians 5:23; Colossians 3:12; James 1:12).

9) **Self-control** – is the restraining of passions and appetites (see 1 Corinthians 9:25; 2 Peter 1:5-6).

Because of the easy accessibility of the gifts of the Spirit, there exists a tendency of many local churches to emphasize the gifts at the expense of the fruit of the Spirit. This is seen very readily in many of the younger churches and ministries. While it poses an extremely dangerous threat to the next generation of churches, too many present-day churches are swayed that way. One reason many believers prefer that *substitution* of the gifts and good works [institutional religion] for the fruit of the Spirit – is the fact that the fruit must be cultivated and cared for requiring much time, effort, and discipline. Whereas the gifts are given by the Holy Spirit severally as He wills. While some fruit may seem to be easier to develop than others, we must remember that we are commanded to develop all of the fruit!

These are the fruit of the Spirit, not the gifts of the Spirit which were covered in an earlier section (see again: Romans 12:6-8 and 1 Corinthians 12:8-10). There is a difference between the fruit of the Spirit and the gifts of the Spirit:

- Again, the gifts of the Spirit are *bestowed* on believers by grace as it pleases God, the Holy Spirit to give them.
- The means of acquiring the fruit of the Spirit, are quite different. Fruit [Christlike character] must be *cultivated,* and that requires much time and effort. Ample cost is involved in the development of the fruit of the Spirit.

This is why many Christians operate in the gifts, but do not give any evidence of having the fruit of the Sprit, Christlikeness. Many simply are not willing to pay the price to produce that fruit. Some are even trying to redefine Christlikeness. This is also the reason many Christians who serve and function in the gifts even under a tremendous anointing, can be some of the rudest people you have ever met – is that alright? Christians who operate in these gifts may perform miraculous signs and wonders, but that does not ensure that they will possess the character of Jesus Christ.

Putting more emphasis on the gifts at the expense of the fruit of the Spirit is extremely dangerous because the main purpose of the gifts is to produce the fruit. In Mark 4:28,29 Jesus said,

> *"For the earth bringeth forth fruit of herself; first the blade, then the ear, after that the full corn in the ear. But when the fruit is brought forth, immediately he putteth in the sickle, because the harvest is come."* KJV

We know that the development of fruit is a growth process even as taught in the laws of nature. Think of an orange tree like all fruit bearing trees begins as a mere blade or flower. This is also true in the spiritual realm. Every believer is a "fruit tree." Take the orange for example, although it has a number of slices it takes all of the slices to make one whole orange.

The word fruit is one of those words that can be used in the singular or plural. Like the orange, the fruit of the Spirit in the spiritual realm has nine parts, but it takes all of them to make-up the *one* fruit of the Spirit. If you peel the orange and divide it into slices, some slices are more developed or larger than others. The same is true with developing the fruit of the Spirit, for example:

- One person may have been cultivating the fruit of gentleness in his or her life, and that fruit may be largely developed; whereas in another person the fruit of gentleness is not as well developed, because he has been developing the fruit of faith.
- It is the persons who have developed *all* of their fruit who will be *most* mature and manifest. For the believer it means all of the *fruit of the Spirit* (manifesting the character of Christ).
- Believers cannot become selective so they can develop only those fruit that offer the least resistance to their personality or their flesh. One might say, "I choose to develop the fruit of faith, but not the fruit of long suffering." Believers must develop all of the fruit. For no part is optional.

Jesus Christ is coming back for a people conformed to His image. Thus, every believer must be striving to develop a hundredfold, all the fruit of the Spirit, for Jesus Himself was a hundredfold – not thirtyfold or sixtyfold, instead His life bore one hundredfold all nine parts of the one whole fruit!

Our spiritual development and production should never stop! When considering spiritual growth, we must realize the truth of (I Corinthians 3:5,6) *that it is always God Who gives the increase.* The Word of God clearly explains how to develop each (part) of the fruit of the Spirit.

The Lord gives believers unique arenas in which to fulfill their giftedness, and He provides **apostolic anointing, and power** to energize them and accomplish them (Romans 12:6; Acts 1:8).

A point to remember: The Word of God transforms us, but that can not happen if you are not informed. Paul starts by saying:

"Now about spiritual gifts brethren, I do not want you to be ignorant"
(see 1 Corinthians 12:1).

A mighty army (the anointed apostolic)

The more I know of our troubled local churches the more I feel like the two recruits on the deck of a troop ship gazing out at the Atlantic for the first time. One said, "Man, look at all that water!" "Yeah, and that isn't all, said the other." "You're just looking at the top of it." Most people have no clue as to what the depth of the conflict that is taking place in so many local churches, we are just looking at the top of it.

Believers must be committed to Jesus Christ and His teachings (doctrine) as recorded in the Scriptures. We must know what we believe and why we believe it. If *love* is the distinguishing mark of a Christian, are we not commanded to live together in peace and unity? (Carefully do a personal study Romans 7:19-20; James 4:1; 2 Corinthians 2:11).

Some conflicts come into the church because we have adopted so many of the world's behaviors, practices, and standards as permissible – overlooking or denying the truth of God's Word. For example, some local churches look at their pastor as a chief operating officer. They hire a pastor to produce what they want [much is undisclosed] and when he or she does not do so, the pastor is fired.

There are some pastors who see themselves as a corporate executive with total authority over the congregation. Finally, there are the hirelings, in it for the money. There are so many poor examples – we need the manifestation of the apostolic *ministry* and *sons* of God to bring about Christlike examples – as Christ so vividly demonstrated during His walk here on the earth.

As earlier stated, the Book of Acts is the only unfinished book in the New Testament, [it continues being written today in the church] but how can it be finished after we have killed off [denied] the essential characters? Most of our gutted churches leave so little for the Holy Spirit and His ministries to work with.

Sadly, much of what we are doing in our local churches is wrong and we know that it is wrong. Yet we perpetuate that wrongness by continuing to teach and train each new generation to do the same!

Jay Leach

The Cadre (God's *Spirit-filled* Captains)

However, all is not lost. The true sons of God can manifest, but only as every believer loves God and comes into the knowledge of the truth and commit themselves to a personal relationship with Him! We must welcome the Holy Spirit and His gifts and ministries. Then, we must stop denying certain parts of Scripture, for whatever reason. For example, some denominations and churches deny the use of apostles, prophets, and the teachers today [the Antioch model], yet their functions are so needed in the body of Christ (see Ephesians 4:11). Another is the denial of the gifts of healings (see 1 Corinthians 12:9).

In the nineties the apostle was restored to the church. As stated elsewhere in this work, the five ministers of Ephesians 4:11 were given to the body of Christ by Christ on His ascension, to provide an apostolic leadership team.

Restoration of the saints (God's *Spirit-filled* soldiers)

This is necessary and must be done if we are going to manifest sons of God to the world. In 1 Cor.12:1-11 we read:

> *There are diversities of gifts, but the same Spirit. There are differences of ministries, but the same Lord. And there are diversities of activities, but it is same God who works all in all. But the manifestation of the Spirit is given to each one for the profit of all: for to one is given the word of wisdom through the Spirit, to another the word of knowledge through the same Spirit, to another faith by the same Spirit, to another gifts of healings by the same Spirit, to another the working of miracles, to another prophecy, to another different kinds of tongues, to another the interpretation of tongues. But one and the same Spirit works all these things, distributing to each one individually as He wills.*

When the sons of God present a proper hearing, believing and application of the gospel a person will see the need to be rescued from a situation that is totally hopeless and impossible to achieve in their own strength and abilities. The Bible announces the kind of rescue the individuals need; and the gospel provides the means to get it – to accomplish this apostolic objective, Christ is working to complete the Great Commission, through mobilizing the sons of God [true saints] from local churches around the world. The church must shift its priorities to *discipleship* without giving up the ministries and missions to those persons already reached.

Some people are giving up their responsibilities in the churches in order to minister too people outside of the church. Persecution will come from fellow members of the church. Some of these disciples have been labeled "unfaithful" to the church or "not committed. It is a sad day when answering the call to duty earns you the ridicule of the church. Apostolic values are:

- About establishing initiatives in the streets (evangelism/ church plants
- People's needs
- Breaking down barriers
- Community issues (God's work in people)
- A home and foreign policy (missional)

Anyone who has tried to lead a church from a club to a disciple-making body can tell you this of the experience:

- They can tell you how their stigmata were received at the hands of club members.
- There is resistance to apostolic discipleship values even in churches that are reaching people.
- Why is this? Well, if their growth is occurring because they offer the best church game in town – club members values usually or dominant.
- Just start talking about reducing time in church so members can have more time to invest in the community and how fast that suggestion can chill the room.
- Club members are not interested in developing relationships outside the club.

- Just begin offering tickets to the annual Christmas dinner to only those who will bring the unsaved with them. Boy did the howl go up!
- Start reducing the activities for club members.
- Start partnering with other believers from other churches to establish community ministry initiatives.
- You will find out how entrenched club members values are.

An apostolic church culture will need to begin prioritizing initiatives such as those in the preceding paragraph above. Christ *alone* is bearing our sins and guilt to Calvary! That is our motivation. Give Him praise and glory!

CHAPTER ELEVEN

ORIENTED TOWARD OTHERS

"Go therefore and make disciples of all nations, baptizing them in the name of the father and of the Son and of the Holy Spirit, teaching them to observe all things that I have commanded you; and lo, I am with you always, even to the end of the age"(Matthew 28:18-20).

As Jesus ended His time on earth, He *commanded* His disciples to "make disciples" (Matthew 28:18-20)! He taught them to live in view not of today or tomorrow – but eternity. In *obedience* to His command, we try to help others follow Jesus; we proclaim God's Word, and we pray for gospel influence, that we may see fruit. Our goal of discipleship is always to present people *mature* in Christ! Christ is working to complete the Great Commission, through mobilizing the apostolic and the sons of God [true saints] from local churches around the world. Paul admonishes, "Speak the truth in love so that your church will become mature:" *"till we all come to the unity of the faith and of the knowledge of the Son of God to a perfect man, to the measure of the fulness of Christ.' But speaking the truth in love, may grow up in all things into Him, who is the Head – Christ"* (Ephesians 4:13, 15).

What is a disciple?

The Greek term for "disciple" in the New Testament is *mathetes*, which means more than just a "student" or "learner." Before we can disciple others, we must be a disciple following Christ ourselves. A disciple is one who not only follows, Jesus, but has entered into a personal saving relationship with Him. You have been, *"united with Christ"* through the New Covenant in His blood.

You have been united through the New Covenant
in His blood. Through His death and resurrection,
He has taken all of your sins and guilt and given
you His righteousness (Philippians 2:1-11).

Jesus Christ is the Good Shepherd who laid His life down for His sheep (John 10:11). So, a Christian *disciple* begins here with the acceptance of this free gift: **1)** grace, **2)** mercy, **3)** a personal relationship with Christ, **4)** eternal life. We accept this gift and join ourselves to Christ and follow by faith. For many American churches including ours at times, "success" is having as many people as possible fill up the worship services on Sundays to hear preaching and teaching from God's Word – adding people to the church. This explains why you hire a church staff to facilitate those services. That is why you need to raise a lot of money from the congregants to fund those salaries. That also explains why buildings are so important. You need a place to have these worship services. And you need much more money from the congregants, often many thousands to millions to build and maintain these facilities. Thus, we see that, embracing this traditional way of doing church costs a lot of money.

After 23 years of pioneering, the Bread of Life Ministries Intl. [BOLM] offers an alternative church model that explains how the apostolic [not to be confused with the Apostolic Denomination]. The Bread of Life does not focus on *adding members* to a church but on *making disciples who will make more disciples* (2 Timothy 2:2).

With Bread of Life, "Disciples form into churches, ministries [intercessors, deliverance, healing and helps] and other ministry teams. We do not plant churches hoping to *get* disciples. Our goal is to obediently *make* disciples, and from those disciple-making *efforts*, churches and ministries are planted." In 1998 we planted the Bread of

Life Christian Center and Church [our flagship church] in Whiteville, NC along with the Bread of Life Bible Institute (also founded in 1998).

We use the Great Commission as the model to highlight the differences between BOLM and more *traditional* church growth models. In the first two words of Matthew 28:19-20, Jesus said, *"therefore go,"* to me, that is saying the big difference between Bread of Life and many churches and more traditional denominational church models. We use the Antioch (Gentile) model of the New Testament Christianity – because of the Jewish nature of the Jerusalem church, and because of the destruction of Jerusalem in A.D. 70. In most other models, in order to reach lost people, the objective is to try to get them to come to church. That is why buildings are so important. You do not primarily go to the lost to make disciples on their turf; you try to get them to come to your church. Jesus seemed to encourage the disciples to focus more on going to the lost than trying to get them to come to you."

It is fair to say that the church at Antioch (a sending church) became the first church to really model true New Testament Christianity. In doing so, it became the pattern for the world. It continues to serve us today as the pattern for an apostolic church. The Antioch church had been birthed out of an apostolic ministry and it went on to fulfill an apostolic call as a congregation. The key elements in the foundation of that church serve as a model for apostolic churches around the world today. Reaching our own Jerusalem is still the first commission to the church (see Acts 1:8). Listed below are twelve characteristics of the N.T. Antioch model today:

1) An Evangelistic Church (see Acts 11:19-20)
2) A Teaching Church (see Acts 11:26; 13:1)
3) A Multi-Racial Church (see Acts 11:20; 13:1)
4) A Team Ministry Church (see Acts 13:1)
5) A Spirit-Anointed Church (see Acts 3:2)
6) A Prophetic Church (see 11:27-30; 13:2)
7) A Generous Church (see Acts 11:30; 13:3)
8) A Worshipping Church (see Acts 13:2)
9) A Praying Church (see Acts 13:3)
10) An Equipping Church (see Ephesians 4:11-12)
11) A World Church (see Acts 15:39-40)
12) A Respected Church (Antioch 1 of the top 5 churches for many centuries to follow.

Next, Jesus said, *"and make disciples,"* I think every pastor in America wants to do this well. I also think most American pastors would admit they are not doing it as well as they would like." The late 20th century church model, in so many applications, requires so much energy and attention that little to nothing is left for anything else – *including discipleship.* The 20th century church model, which revolved around church buildings, weekend gatherings, sermons and the like is not focused primarily on discipleship. Discipleship gets crowded out because doing all of those things take up so much time.

Many pastors want to make disciples well, but it seems like all of the other traditional church activities keeps us so busy we do not have much time to really consider what one theologian had to say, *"In all that we are doing, what are we making? Are we making disciples? Or are we making something else?"*

The next part of the Great Commission Jesus said, "Make disciples *"of all nations."* What Jesus commands in this section is mind boggling to the disciples, they ask the question out loud or under their breath, "Make disciples of <u>all nations?</u> We need to allow the Holy Spirit to guide us in imagining how the first disciples heard this straight from Jesus Himself. Historical records reflect about two million people in all the nations of the known world at that time. Jesus was saying in essence, "I want you to go and make disciples of all of them. What?

But Jesus told them how, "They would have to make disciples, who make more disciples, who make more disciples up to four generations. If they would *multiply disciples* rather than *depend on addition.* In essence they could reach whole nations. That is vastly different from the traditional church model – which simply seeks to start a church, hire a preacher, buy or rent a building eventually and just hope it grows. There is absolutely no initial aim usually to reach an entire city, region, or nation.

In the American model, generally, we do not encourage ordinary, unschooled men like Peter and John to make disciples and plant churches.

It takes a disciple to make a disciple.

We leave that for the professionals. I was not a pastor exceptionally long before I realized that the philosophy of ministry described above was a great hindrance to the multiplication of disciples. In founding

Bread of Life twenty-two years ago, I felt just the opposite and used Holy Spirit-filled men and women after we had equipped them through the Bread of Life Bible Institute and Church which I founded with my wife Magdalene in August 1998. Jesus further commanded his disciples in the Great Commission to, *"To teach them [new disciples] to obey all the things He has commanded them."* Our focus was not just on learning or the accumulation of knowledge – it was on obedience to Jesus Christ. Bread of Life is an apostolic ministry a *radical* new, Spirit-empowered definition of ministry success. Success is not measured by buildings, budgets, or attendance. It is measured by whether disciples and churches are multiplying to the fourth generation and beyond such that whole people groups can be reached." By now it must be obvious why BOLM has proven to be such a strong and effective method for evangelism and discipleship. "Multiplication always grows more quickly than addition and thus has the potential to reach whole cities, regions, and nations." I am not saying that addition is bad or not helpful. You can reach a lot of people through addition – but nothing like what you can reach through multiplication." Radical? Yes! Radical for Jesus. Yes! The Apostolic is Rising you better get on board! All for His glory.

CHAPTER TWELVE

APOSTOLIC TIMES

And when they had prayed, the place where they were assembled together was shaken; and they were all filled with the Holy Spirit, and they **spoke** *the word of God* **with boldness** (Acts 4:31).

Every generation and age need pioneers. Humans tend to remain the same and sometimes even revert backward. The church is no exception and the Lord Himself has provided the apostolic anointing to keep the church on the cutting edge. It pushes us forward toward fulfillment of our commission. It keeps the church from being outmoded and outdated, by releasing us from the past and thrusting us into the future in the present. It makes the church relevant to our world without compromise.

God's pioneers

Apostles are pioneers. Paul was a founder and foundation layer. The early apostles laid the foundation of the church (see I Corinthians 3:10). Every movement in the Church has had foundation layers. It enables us to meet the challenges of a changing world. Martin Luther laid the foundation for the Reformation (1517). William Seymour laid the foundation for the Pentecostal Movement (1906). Every generation needs this kind of people, it is quite evident we need them today – otherwise nothing will be established. Without the apostolic dimension a whole generation can be lost. Perhaps we have already lost more than one generation, while the bickering continues as to whether or not the apostleship was ended. Again, I remind you the five ministers (dimensions) of Ephesians 4:11 are to be here until?

The apostolic Flow

The apostolic anointing flows from Jesus through the apostle, prophet, evangelist, pastor, and teacher to the saints worldwide. Each anointing is unique and serves a unique and important purpose and each has certain characteristics. *If* the Church receives all five functions by being exposed to anointed ministry gifts – it can manifest Christ to the world. All five gifts together manifest Christ's fullness.

We are putting a lot of emphasis on the apostolic dimension because it is so necessary for the local church to function properly – therefore, each local church must develop a strategy for accessing apostolic grace. There are two ways a local church can accomplish this:

1) One Way is to have an apostle as the senior elder (pastor) of the local church. Apostles can pastor because there is a shepherding dimension to the apostolic anointing. When the senior elder is an apostle, there will be a *consistent flow* of the apostolic anointing that will cause a strong apostolic dimension to be present in the local church – which is released *through the preaching, teaching, prophesying, and overall ministry.*

However, all pastors are not apostles. It is not necessary to be an apostle to pastor a local church. Although all pastors are not apostles, all pastors need the apostolic dimension to operate effectively in their ministries in the local churches.

2) The second way for a local church to access apostolic grace is to be in relationship with an apostle. Through this relationship the

apostolic anointing can flow into the local church, releasing an apostolic dimension.

This does not mean an apostolic dimension will come into a local church just because *some of those in the church know an apostle.* There must be a strategy, a course of action that will result in accessing the grace that rests upon the apostolic office. This can include fellowship, conferences, and other means to draw from the anointing upon the apostles with whom pastors are in covenant.

Picture if you will the disciples frightened and discouraged after the crucifixion hiding in closed room for fear of the Jews – could they without *grace,* fulfill the commission given to them by our Lord? Not only did they need grace for the "Impossible Mission" assigned but they needed an *abundance* of grace:

> *And with great power the apostles gave witness to the resurrection of the Lord Jesus. And* **great grace** *was upon them all* (Acts 4:33).

The 120 people from the Upper Room would turn the world upside down. How did this small group of nobodies accomplish the impossible? They did it through *grace.* So, grace defined is the ability of God to do [through us] what ordinarily could not be done. They were recipients of "great grace." The word great in the Greek is translated *"mega"* from which we get our commonly used prefix "mega" meaning exceptionally large in size. The apostles had "mega grace."

The Apostolic Anointing

In Acts 10, We see Cornelius' strategy or course of action, *prayer* and *giving* coming up as a memorial before the Lord. The Lord sent an angel to Cornelius to connect with Peter, who in turn would give him the Word of salvation. Again, the two things that opened the way was prayer and giving. Therefore, prayer and giving is a good strategy to access apostolic grace. As local churches pray for these divine connections, the Lord will *supernaturally* bring these relationships into being.

Do not go after the first person who calls himself or herself an apostle – pray for Cornelius' strategy. Once the connection has been established, releasing finances through giving is one way to access the grace necessary to receive the apostolic dimension. Remember the apostles' mission is impossible? There was no way a group of frightened and discouraged disciples to accomplish it – but the abundance of grace did manifest!

The apostolic anointing releases large amounts of grace to the to the church (see 1 Corinthians 1:4-7). I can say, "Amen to that!" Churches under this anointing will receive all the gifts and abilities it needs to fulfill the Great Commission. Without this great grace, the church will not be able to finish the work. The Great Commission is an *end-time* commission. Never have the means been available to the church to accomplish this end-time commission mandate as they are today. We have the technology, transportation, and finances needed to accomplish the mission. The Lord began to move me into apostolic ministry some years ago as an apostolic pastor and Bible teacher in the Antioch mode [a sending church] (see Acts 11:21, 22).

Antioch a sending Church

The church at Antioch had an apostolic dimension – which was strengthened by the arrival of Barnabas from Jerusalem. Antioch became a teaching center after Barnabas brought Paul to assemble the believers there for an entire year (see Acts 11:26). The church at Antioch was a church filled with grace (see Acts 11:23). This church also became a place where *prophets* and *teachers* ministered (see Acts 13:1). As they ministered to the Lord and fasted, the Holy Spirit instructed them to separate Barnabas and Saul for the ministry of apostleship. Then, having *fasted* and *prayed, laid hands on them, they* **sent** *them away* (acts 13:3).

The church of Antioch became a *sending church*. Barnabas and Paul were sent forth as apostles (sent ones) from Antioch. From Antioch was launched one of the greatest apostolic ministries of all times. As a result of the sending forth Barnabas and Saul – later, Silas and Paul – hundreds of churches were planted all over the known world. The apostolic ministry is team ministry. Antioch became a spiritual hub for apostles, prophets, and teachers. There was a conducive atmosphere for the Spirit of God to separate and release ministries into the world.

Apostolic churches will have an apostolic spirit. The Holy Spirit is an apostolic Spirit. He is sent by the Father, and He sends ministries. Notice, Antioch is an example of a sending church operation in a strong apostolic dimension (see Acts 13:4). Praise God! Barnabas and Saul were *sent* forth by the church and by the Holy Spirit. The Holy Spirit works in conjunction with the Church in sending ministries, the sent ones [Eph. 4:11] are successful ministries because they have the backing of the Church and the Lord.

Home and Foreign Missions

Missions must be a high priority in apostolic churches and apostolic ministries because that is a part of the apostolic mandate (see Acts 13:47). We are called to help existing churches and ministries in other nations; therefore, every church should have a foreign policy. Home missions (USA) should be established to help the saints and plant new churches. Apostolic churches and ministries have a great responsibility to use and distribute the wealth that the apostolic anointing draws. To whom much is given, much is required (Luke 12:48).

Apostolic Times

There are times of reformation that are *predestined* by the Lord. There are also times of release of the apostolic anointing to bring about the *changes ordained by the Lord:*

- Religious systems that have been in place for many years prior to a reformation are *the greatest enemies* to a new move of God.
- Religious systems that need reform serve the *interest of the leadership* of that system. And they are usually a reformation's greatest opponents.

During the days of Jesus and the early apostles, the Pharisees had much to lose in a reformation: their position, power and control *over* the people. The early apostles were *persecuted* by these leaders in order to prevent their completion of a reformation. Reformation is not new.

These same hinderances are serving the same purposes for the leadership [same motives] in many local churches today. Perhaps that was the motivation for the removal of the offices of the apostle, prophet, and teacher. Relics of the times prior to – the Protestant Reformation of 1517, remain in many local churches today. Luxurious facilities many of which I believe will have to be mission-modified after going through the present reformation. The Church is now experiencing *another reformation,* and that means <u>God is working changes in His people</u> – changes that affect every area of our lives specifically: the way we think, or our *mind-sets.*

A time of Reformation is a season of revolutionary change. It is a radical process involving amendment, correction, rectification, renovation, recovery, salvation, rescue and deliverance.

The Lord is preparing the Church to complete its task, and the apostolic ministry is the essential to prepare the Church for this purpose. Without the apostolic ministers of Ephesians 4:11, the Church will lack the necessary *grace, power, and authority* to finish its mission.

In Acts 20:22-24, notice Paul's attitude. He is determined to finish his course. Nothing could dissuade him from completing his ministry. *There was a drive and a determination to finish.* This must be the "mind set" of the Church of the Lord Jesus Christ in every generation! We must have an apostolic mind-set; we must be driven and determined to complete the Great Commission. <u>This mindset overcomes all obstacles and hindrances that stand in the way of finishing</u>. As you charge up the hill toward victory, remember the Pharisees and Sadducees and how Jesus described them.

Trials, tests, and tribulations do not deter the true apostolic ministry. There is an *abundance of grace* resident within this anointing that overcomes all opposition and breaks through every barrier. And it does not cease until the task is complete!

Again, change is uncomfortable – but necessary!

Apostolic Boldness

In the midst of persecution, we have apostolic boldness. Apostolic reformers, [change agents] are noted for their *boldness* in preaching the truth in spite of persecution and even death. Intimidation is another tool the devil uses to stop reformation. The Church's mission is to spread the Gospel of salvation, sacrificial love and ultimate hope that Jesus commissioned His disciple's followers to proclaim. It is not about numeric growth; that is just a by-product – it is about *the good news*. Losing cultural ground is presents a major problem. But losing the gospel – that is a different story!

Some church leaders seem to believe there was absolutely no spiritual guidance before their particular denomination, belief system, church polity or traditions were formed and therefore, like old Israel, they place these tenets above the very Word of God. Have we forgotten that the first church was apostolic? Have we forgotten that it was this church wherein salvation experiences, baptisms, healings, deliverances, and even some were raised from the dead? Have we forgotten it was this church that loved one another [agape] so that it was reported they had all things common? It was this church that it was said, "They turned the world upside down!" The Book of Acts and the Letters are where our blood-washed church's story should be found. Two thousand years later, we are still writing the Book of Acts.

Institutional religious *systems* and their leaders who desire to maintain the *status quo* for their own benefit will use threats against apostolic reformers/ ministers. But apostolic reformers have the anointing and boldness to bring about reform in the face of staunch opposition. They are *hated* and *called* troublemakers because of their message, but they bring to the Church what it needs most – Reformation!

If we are going to pay attention to Jesus' admonition to His disciples, we will not see a restoration of true apostolic ministry to the church – until we can deal effectively with *the desire for preeminence in the hearts of men*. Then and only then will we be able to accept the *biblical definition* of an apostolic ministry. If we find out the ministry of the apostolic is a position that *requires a death to the self – a life of humility: humble service and sacrifice, and a willingness to be discredited for the sake of the Gospel,* we might not be so eager to see it restored. An apostolic is to be a servant above all things, as Jesus modeled to His disciples by washing their feet at the Last Supper (see John 13:7).

Check the records of Paul and Peter, neither had any delusions of greatness when it came to apostolic ministry. Paul understood what it meant to be an apostle. He realized that he was a servant first. He viewed it as more or less a sentence of death (see 2 Corinthians 1:9). Likewise, Peter understood that he was a servant first and an apostle second (see 2 Peter 1:1). When he wrote to the *elders* of the church – he wrote as a *fellow elder.* As you look over the church scene today, there are many who are using the term "apostle" for their own gain. Christian publications are filled with leadership conferences where apostolic ministers are present. In many cases they are using the term in a very Scriptural manner. Unfortunately, there are times where the apostle appears to be elevated above the other ministries in the body of Christ [not Scripturally grounded].

"It seems difficult to me that someone would even consider the Bread of Life Ministries [Apostolic], unless they have first considered Luke 14 and found the following: Jesus is worth any cost! Bread of Life Ministries is an Apostolic Ministry. Being so may require us to give up some things we have always cherished. It may expose competing allegiances or even *idols* that we have worshipped in the place of God. We are a people with character flaws. We are not complete yet, but Christ is mercifully molding and making us like His Son [that is transformation] folks! But our Church has found, and I have found in my personal experience with God – that Jesus continues to be worth it all. He loves us – warts and all. If following Him costs me my life, my comfort, my security or my church *traditions,* He is worth it, and I will gladly surrender all to Jesus – He is the greatest treasure!"

A Charge to Keep I Have

A charge to keep I have – A God to glorify, Who gave His Son my soul to save – And fit it for the sky, To serve the present age – My calling to fulfill, O may it all my pow'rs engage – to do my Master's will.

Charles Wesley
Amen!

BIBLICAL INDEX OF REFERENCES

Printed in the United States
By Bookmasters